The Bob Mover Jazz Lexicon

A Thesaurus of Musical Vocabulary for All Instruments

∽ Second Edition: Bass Clef ∽

By Bob Mover
and Isaac Raz

Editor of the Second Edition: Don Smith

© 2024 Sher Music Co., P.O. Box 445, Petaluma, CA, 94953

All Rights Reserved. International Copyright Secured. Made in the U.S.A.
No part of this book may be reproduced in any form without written permission from the publisher.
979-8-99222-63-0-0

Cover photo: ©Jean-Baptiste Millot
Cover artwork: Paul Klee, "Red Balloon" (detail), Wikimedia Commons
Cover design: Linda McLaughlin

To the memory of

Alvin "Big Al" Heintzleman, who brought Isaac and I together

Michael Brecker, with whom I've spent countless hours practicing and developing these ideas

The Bob Mover Jazz Lexicon
Second Edition: Bass Clef
TABLE of CONTENTS

Endorsements	Inside Front Cover
Title page	i
To the Memory of	ii
Table of Contents	iii
Foreword by Randy Brecker	iv
Introduction	v
Acknowledgments	vi
How to Use this Book	viii
Synopsis	ix
About the Authors	x
LIST OF EXERCISE TITLES	A–J
EXERCISES 1-407	1–85

Foreword by Randy Brecker

Bob Mover is at the top of the Alto Saxophone pantheon; yet, despite many great recordings and gigs never quite gets the recognition by critics (and the general public) he surely deserves. However, he is certainly recognized by fellow musicians and the truly hip cognoscenti (!) so hopefully this book of phrases and ideas from his unique mind will help to change all that.

Charlie Parker, Sonny Rollins, Lee Konitz, Phil Woods are in Bob's DNA, but he's clearly his own man. These 400 or so motifs and patterns are the result of a lifetime of internalizing things he's heard in his head and worked out live on gigs during his over-half-a-century long career (playing with his own groups as well as with the likes of Chet Baker, Charles Mingus, Ira Sullivan, Walter Davis Jr., and Jaki Byard, among many others). His many years spent teaching at the University level also helped solidify his pedagogical methods. This book is very well thought out, with a clearly defined preface and a 'how to' page to help musicians utilize the material to its fullest extent. Additionally, accompanying audio examples corresponding to each exercise are available online to check out.

Besides 'content', Bob's artistry is also defined by his sound and (maybe most importantly) his deep swing. I would highly recommend anyone to check out his recordings and become familiar with his overall approach. I recently spoke to Bob on the phone. He played me a couple of examples, and it sounded like he was standing next to me in my own living room. That's how strong the Music of Bob Mover presents itself. I trust this book will always be sitting on your music stand, or on the desktop of your computer; that you will partake of the myriad of ideas presented here daily, and that your playing and overall musicianship will attain levels you haven't yet imagined.

Deserving kudos and a big thanks to Isaac Raz for helping Bob put this amazing "Jazz Lexicon" together.

—Randy Brecker
2/26/23

Introduction

In 2013, I was diagnosed with emphysema. On several occasions in the ensuing years, I experienced exacerbations so severe that I had to be hospitalized. I'd spend a week or two in the hospital and then come home and continue my life as before. In 2021 I had an attack so severe that I needed to have a tracheostomy performed. I'm happy to say that I did recover and am once again able to play my saxophone. However, this unfortunate event forced me to spend four months in hospitals, two months in the ICU followed by two more months in a rehab facility.

I had never before in my life spent four months away from my horns. I was fortunate in that I knew how to practice without my instrument. I had learned this from years of touring—being on the road in trains and planes, airports and train stations where I had to prepare for an imminent gig in a matter of hours, with only a little time to get my reed wet and play the concert.

While physically immobile during my recovery I did lots of this "mental practicing." I played tunes in different keys as I worked out the changes and "imagined" the sound. Sometimes I would finger the notes on my imaginary horn, sometimes I just played in my head. Besides songs, I practiced many of the exercises and musical "patterns" that I had worked on during my half a century of playing music. Some related to scales and arpeggios, some purely intervallic.

I faithfully and diligently practiced these "snippets." The hours spent daily in this activity saved, if not my life, at least my sanity during this spiritually trying time.

When I came back home after being released from rehab I began to write down these ideas at the pace of a few per day. Within a month or so I had notated nearly all of the 400+ examples found in this book.

When I showed what I had done to my colleague, Isaac Raz, he enthusiastically told me that he felt I had created something that would be of lasting value to, not only jazz, but to the whole genre of musical pedagogy.

Isaac then proceeded to transfer the scratchiness of my original scrawl into the beautifully formatted version that you now have in front of you. He also played and recorded on synthesizer examples of each pattern, thus enabling the user to listen to them. My thanks to Isaac for his precise and industrious efforts.

Acknowledgments

To: My Mentors,

Ira Sullivan, Joe Diorio, Dolph and Tony Castellano, Phil Woods, Jerry Coker, Wynton Kelly, Kenny Dorham, Stan Getz, Lee Konitz, Jaki Byard, Sonny Rollins, Chet Baker, Zoot Sims, Walter Davis Jr., Art Farmer, James Moody, Duke Jordan, Junior Cook, Sal Nistico, Jimmy Mosher, Richie Kamuca, Roy Eldridge, Al Cohn, Clifford Jordan, Steve Lacy, Paul Bley, Kenny Barron, Gordon Brisker, Bill Rubenstein, Joe Kaercher, and the many others who taught me the Craft and how to use it to make Art.

And to my many dear friends, for the many hours we have spent inspiring each other: Mike Brecker, Al Dailey, Tom Harrell, Hal Galper, Mike Gerber, Jerry Bergonzi, Brooks Kerr, Steve Hall, Bob Berg, Dave Liebman, David Valdez, and Claudio Roditi.

A very special acknowledgment of gratitude to Steve Kenyon, for his over 40 years of dedication to my musical endeavors and lending his time, great talent, energy and patience in contributing to the creation of the Lexicon.

Thanks to Randy Brecker for writing his excellent Preface.

Special Thanks to my wonderful wife, Yvonne, for her ever present love and caring; to my amazing daughters, Emilie, Anya and Simona for the joy and inspiration that they constantly bring to my life; to my siblings Richard and Joy Mover for being there for me from the beginning; and Isaac Raz, for his integral insights and hours of work in making this book happen.

Lastly, my deepest thanks to Chuck Sher for bringing this book out to the world.

"Improvising is like digging holes, no matter how brilliant the holes you dig are, the real trick is how you get out of them."
   —Lee Konitz

"Try to swing, and find the pretty notes."
   — Chet Baker

"You have to look at the big picture, most people think in snapshots".
   —Sonny Rollins

"We all have a light inside of us, and the whole thing is to get closer to that light."
   —Barry Harris

How to Use this Book

The first time I was presented with the concept of "Patterns" was when I was 15 and studying with the great Phil Woods. Phil gave me a copy of Oliver Nelson's "Patterns for Saxophone" (now titled "Patterns for Jazz"[2]) as a present. He encouraged me to not just play them on the horn but to play them on piano as well.

He liked the fact that Mr. Nelson had not specified any chord changes that fit the patterns and had left it up to the user to find the harmonic possibilities. With the exception of a few instances where some chords are given, this Lexicon works in the same way.

There is a **List of Exercise Titles** providing a description of each example.

In using these motifs it is important that the user keep in mind that they are not an end in themselves, for there are few things more boring than listening to a musician who's playing is nearly entirely made up of academic pyrotechnics. I have tried to use these ideas in the spirit of the Zen Master who said, "When pointing one's finger at the moon one should never mistake the finger for the moon." They should be used as a way to increase your proficiency on your instrument while expanding your ears.

Another Zen Master, albeit an American who lived in Queens, Lennie Tristano once said to me, "People talk about playing what you hear. Well, I'm not interested in teaching that. I want to teach you to play what you don't hear!"

In this sense I would wish that these exercises might serve to assist you, the student, in constantly expanding to another level of musical understanding and coherent expression.

Here is a summary of the types of patterns used and some suggested ways to practice them:

1) *Chromatically:* Most of these ideas, no matter how they are presented, can be played in half steps up and down from any place on your instrument. *[Editor: under this heading we have grouped patterns which are —*
   A: Essentially Chromatic
   B: Scalic
   C: Chordal/Arpeggiated]

2) *Whole Steps:* Specific ideas based on the whole tone scale, augmented scale, and major 3rd patterns are, most often, just written in one position. It is left to the user to place the motif correctly into the other starting places.*

3) *Minor 3rds and Diminished:* Can all be played from three positions, each containing four minor thirds. As with Whole Tones, the students are provided with one example and left to make the other necessary transpositions for themselves.

4) *Cyclic:* Can be played from 12 positions in the cycle of 5ths or the cycle of 4ths from anywhere on the instrument. *[Editor: this approach can be adopted for most of the exercises in The Jazz Lexicon. Under this heading we have grouped those demonstrating characteristic chord progressions]*

5) *Tritones (Flatted 5ths):* From 6 places.

---

[2] "Patterns for Improvisation" by Oliver Nelson. New Albany, IN: Jamey Aebersold Jazz, 2015.

Editor: Bob has also shared samples of his exercises exploring two characteristic harmonic structures, namely —

    6) *Dominant 7ths:* These can apply to their usual functional role in a progression or to extended passages for improvisation.

    7) *Quartals:* Harmonic structures based on the interval of a fourth.

Think of the notes slowly, key by key. If you do this right you won't have to think for long. It is not exactly "playing by ear" because you follow the same process for just about everything. This is my way of applying Adolf Sandole's "playing by mind" idea.

Here is an example of the thought process:

1. Key of . . . (?)
2. Number and names of sharps and flats
3. What is the anatomy of the pattern?

    A) All diatonic
    B) Diatonic with chromatic embellishment
    C) Purely intervallic with no reference to any particular key

With these ideas in mind, the student can then absorb the "big picture" of this book's intention, and apply it to his or her musical growth.

There are some audio examples included within. All examples of the content have been recorded on synthesizer and there are 18 examples of patterns being played by Bob Mover on Alto, both individually and with keyboard accompaniment on familiar chord progressions. Audio files are available on the Sher Music CD Downloads page, https://www.shermusic.com/new/downloads.shtml and also the book's webpage, https://www.shermusic.com/9780991077328.php.

    —Bob Mover

Synopsis

The Jazz Lexicon deals with musical logic that makes up the vocabulary of the modern jazz language. It is stimulating for musicians at all levels to learn how the ideas that form musical sequences are constructed. These scale, arpeggio and interval formulas, patterns and permutations lead the instrumentalist (and composer) to hear ideas that they didn't hear before, and to incorporate these ideas into their improvisations and compositions. Consistent practice of even some of the 400+ examples included here, played in all keys, are guaranteed to train your ear and your fingers to work together and help you reach new levels of harmonic and melodic understanding.

About the Authors

Bob Mover, born in 1952, started playing alto saxophone at 13 and quickly impressed Phil Woods, earning a scholarship at 15 to Woods' Summer Jazz camp. He learned from jazz legends like Roy Eldridge, Kenny Dorham, Jaki Byard and Ira Sullivan, later joining Charles Mingus and Chet Baker's groups. Collaborations with Lee Konitz and Walter Davis Jr. followed, leading to acclaimed albums like "In the True Tradition." Throughout his career, Mover taught, toured, and recorded extensively, recently founding Lower Manhattan Music Studio and continuing his jazz education efforts with "Bob Mover JazzAbility" and his podcast "On the Real Side."

Isaac Raz is a graduate of Berklee College Of Music in jazz composition and music synthesis under the tutelage of Herb Pomeroy, where he received the Duke Ellington award. He holds a Master of Arts in Teaching degree from Lehman College, City University of New York. Isaac has received further mentoring with the great Barry Harris for over a decade, and as a colleague of Bob Mover. In addition to helping him with this book, Isaac created full orchestrations for Bob's upcoming orchestral album. Isaac has also arranged and produced tracks for Teo Macero's "Impressions of Miles Davis" album, and composed the score for the Emmy award-winning television documentary "Pioneer Women." His latest orchestration project for Antoine Drye, "Retreat to Beauty" was just released on Cellar Music.

Isaac is the founder and president of Whole Music LLC teaching all over the world, and continues composing, producing and arranging for media.

Don Smith is a trombonist living in Sydney, Australia. It was his idea to have us publish a bass clef version. During the process of engraving the music for that book he suggested reorganizing the material to put similar exercises together. We feel it is a real improvement over the first edition so we have created a Second Edition for the treble clef version as well. Thanks, Don!

The Bob Mover Jazz Lexicon
Second Edition: Bass Clef

List of Exercise Titles

Section 1A: Chromatic 1

    1: Triplets with descending chromatics, moving in 4ths
    2: Triplets with descending chromatics in 4ths, used on II V I
    3: Same as #2 a major 3rd higher
    4: Three chromatics a 4th apart
    5: Chromatic ascending triplets, descending in half steps
    6: Chromatic triplet pattern
    7 Perfect 5th phrase with chromatic embellishment, ascending chromatically
    8: Intervallic pattern in tritones (#339), but using "Chromatic Passageway"
    9: Chromatic permutation
    10: Chromatic permutation, ascending in 4ths
    11: Chromatic permutation, descending in 4ths
    12: 4-note chromatic permutation, descending in whole steps
    13: A series of four chromatic triplets, each group descending in whole steps (Dizzy Gillespie)
    14: Ascending chromatic interval pattern using minor 3rds and tritones
    15: Chromatic triplets separated by a tritone, ascending chromatically
    16: Chromatic permutation in descending form, ascending and descending in major 3rds
    17: Chromatic permutation in ascending form, ascending and descending in major 3rds
    18: "Chromatic Passageway" in a major 3rd interval, separated and combined, ascending chromatically
    19: Neighbor note enclosures to the 3rd (Dizzy Gillespie), ascending chromatically
    20: Ascending tritone with lower chromatic neighbors, ascending chromatically
    21: Descending tritone with upper chromatic neighbors, ascending chromatically
    22: Descending tritone with lower chromatic neighbors, ascending chromatically
    23: Ascending minor 6th to descending 5th, descending chromatically

Section 1B: Scalic 6

    24: Dorian with chromatic neighbors on II V ascending in half steps
    25: Same pattern of notes resolving to keys minor 3rds apart
    26: Major scale pattern on 6-5 4-3 9-1 with lower chromatic neighbor notes
    27: Same scale relationships as #26 in ascending pattern
    28: Same scale relationships as #26 in descending pattern
    29: Ascending diatonic triplets in 3rds with chromatic neighbors
    30: Same as #29 but descending
    31: Diatonic scale patterns with diatonic neighbors ascending in minor 3rds over II V I
    32: Scale permutation with alternating neighbors in minor 3rds (Back Door)
    33: First three notes of minor scale in triplets, moving in cycle
    34: Diatonic scale pattern on dominant 7ths, descending in half steps
    35: Pentatonic pattern descending in minor thirds, (in 3 : 4 rhythmic feel)
    36: Four-note lick based on dominant or blues scale, ascending in half steps

37: Diatonic scale permutation descending chromatically
38: Diatonic 6ths with neighbor notes, descending
39: 1 2 3 5 pattern, descending chromatically
40: Diatonic descending scale pattern, modulating in descending half steps
41: Major 6ths with neighbor notes, descending chromatically
42: Major 6ths with neighbor notes, ascending chromatically
43: Diatonic passage with chromatic embellishment, moving in cycle of
44: Major diatonic pattern ascending in whole steps
45: Major diatonic pattern, one up, one down, ascending in half steps (pentatonic)
46: Diatonic pattern descending in major thirds
47: Major to minor phrase using 4ths and 7ths
48: Syncopated phrase ascending chromatically
49: Minor pentatonic phrase, ascending chromatically
50: Bluesy intervallic pattern ascending chromatically
51: Pattern of 3 5 2 flat 2 1, moving in cycle of 5ths.
52: Descending chromatic approach to ascending melodic minor scale, in cycle of 5ths
53: Ascending chromatic approach to descending melodic minor 9th arpeggio, in cycle of 5ths
54: Minor 6ths with chromatic approach, ascending in whole steps
55: Dorian modes ascending from the 9th to the 9th with chromatic neighbor, and descending arpeggio, 9th to 3
56: Chromatic "enclosure" of the 3rd of major, ascending chromatically
57: Blues scale phrase, ascending in half steps
58: Intervallic study on minor
59: Intervallic pattern: Descending 4th with chromatic embellishment, ascending chromatically
60: Inverse of #59
61: "Spirals" on major, ascending chromatically
62: Phrase on melodic minor, descending chromatically

Section 1C: Chords/Arpeggios 15

63: Permutation of major 7ths voiced 3 5 7 6, OR minor 7ths voiced 5 7 9 1, descending in minor 3rds
64: Same as #63 as used on a II V I progression
65: Dorian with chromatic neighbor followed by minor seventh arpeggio ascending chromatically
66: Minor 7th arpeggios with chromatic neighbor, moving through cycle
67: Minor 7th arpeggios with chromatic neighbor ascending in minor 3rds
68: same as #67 but descending in minor 3rds
69: Same as #67 and #68 but ascending in whole steps
70: Minor 7th arpeggios with chromatic neighbor a tritone apart used on II V I
71: Minor 7th arpeggios (ascending form) "Back door" to "Lydian"
72: I major and flat VII triads alternating while ascending in all inversions
73: Diatonic triads descending form with lower chromatic neighbor, ascending the scale
74: Diatonic triads descending form with lower chromatic neighbor, descending the scale
75: A diatonic pattern (3 5 2 1) descending in minor 3rds
76: Minor triads with 9th ascending in half steps
77: 9th chord arpeggios (3 to 9) ascending in minor 3rds
78: Same as #77 but one up, one down

79: Major triads ascending chromatically alternating root position & 3rd inversion (Lester Young)
80: Descending second inversion major triads with flatted 5th on the bottom
81: Same as #80 but descending in half steps
82: Same as #80 but in cycle of 5ths
83: Arpeggiated phrase with chromatic neighbor notes, ascending chromatically
84: Chromatic embellishment on major, moving in cycle of 5ths
85: An inverted major arpeggio pattern ascending in whole steps
86: Triadic patterns moving up keys in whole steps (Lee Konitz)
87: Major triads in second inversion with chromatic neighbors, ascending in half steps
88: Major triads in root position with lower chromatic neighbor, ascending in whole steps
89: Two major triads a half step apart with lower chromatic neighbor, alternating inversions
90: Major triads in second inversion, ascending chromatically
91: Root position triads with upper chromatic neighbor, ascending in half steps
92: Minor triads with chromatic neighbor notes ascending in minor thirds
93: Descending minor triad with upper chromatic neighbor, ascending in minor thirds
94: Lower chromatic neighbor to the 3rd outlining a major chord, ascending chromatically
95: Minor 9ths voiced 3 7 3 9, descending in whole steps
96: Major arpeggio with chromatic neighbor note, ascending in whole steps
97: Minor triads with neighbor notes, ascending in whole steps
98: Minor triads with neighbor notes, descending chromatically
99: Dominant 13th flat9, descending chromatically
100: Major 9th chords (also could be minor pentatonic), ascending chromatically
101: Same as #100, but in inverse
102: Major 7ths, voiced 9 1 3 7, ascending chromatically
103: Same as #102, ascending in minor 3rds
104: Same as #102, descending in minor 3rds
105: Minor 7th chords, with "chromatic passageway", descending in minor 3rds
106: Major 7th arpeggios with neighbor notes, ascending in major 3rds
107: Intervallic triad pattern, descending in whole steps
108: Same as #107, ascending in whole steps
109: A variation on #107, alternating whole steps and tritones
110: Another intervallic triad pattern, descending in whole steps
111: 1st inversion minor triads with lower chromatic neighbor, ascending chromatically
112: 2nd inversion minor triads with lower chromatic neighbor, ascending chromatically
113: Root position minor triads with lower chromatic neighbor, ascending chromatically
114: Same as #113, ascending in whole steps
115: 2nd inversion minor triads with lower chromatic neighbor, descending in whole steps
116: Major 9th chords voiced 5 3 9 7, ascending chromatically
117: Same as #116 adding chromatic approach
118: Descending major 6th arpeggios, ascending in minor 3rds
119: Same as #118, descending in minor 3rds
120: Descending 2nd inversion minor 7th arpeggios, descending chromatically
121: Descending major 9th arpeggios, voiced 5 3 9 maj7, ascending in minor 3rds
122: Same as #121, descending in minor 3rds
123: 1st inversion major triads ascending in major 3rds (symmetric augmented)
124: 1st inversion major triads with lower chromatic neighbor, descending in major 3rds

125: 2nd inversion major triads with lower chromatic neighbor, ascending in major 3rds (symmetric augmented)

126: An arpeggiated -maj7 chord broken into 7ths, spelling 1 7 3 9 11 6, ascending chromatically (Yusef Lateef)

127: Minor 9th with chromatics pattern, ascending in whole steps

128: Minor triads ascending in major 3rds

129: Major triads with added 9ths, ascending and descending in major 3rds

130: Open 5ths with chromatic neighbors in dotted rhythm, ascending chromatically (Hank Mobley, Charlie Parker)

131: Minor 7th arpeggios voiced 7 5 1 3, ascending chromatically

132: Minor 7th arpeggios voiced 9 1 5 7, descending chromatically

133: Arpeggio pattern on V13b9 (Jackie McLean)

134: Pattern of 7th to 3rd of II V, ascending in minor 3rds

135: Same as #134, descending in minor 3rds

136: Permutation of minor 7th chords, ascending chromatically

137: Descending 2nd inversion minor triads, with neighbor notes and 16th note triplets, ascending in whole steps

138: Descending 2nd inversion major triads, with neighbor notes and 16th note triplets, descending in whole steps

139: 2 5 3 1 ascending and descending in major 3rds (Sonny Rollins)

Section 2: Whole Tone/Augmented/Major 3rds 30

140: Permutation of augmented scale

141: Permutation of augmented scale with neighbor notes

142: Permutation of augmented scale, one down, one up

143: Augmented triad permutation (1 3 +5 3) ascending in minor 3rds

144: Augmented triad permutation (3 1 3 +5) ascending in minor 3rds

145: Whole Tone pattern in major thirds (Bud Powell)

146: Ascending augmented triads in minor thirds in quarter note triplets 147: Parallel major thirds pattern (John Coltrane)

147: Parallel major thirds pattern (John Coltrane)

148: Whole steps, descending in half steps

149: Intervallic pattern: major 3rds with double chromatic approach, ascending in half steps

150: Same as #149, but descending in half steps

151: Whole steps ascending chromatically in 16th note triplets

152: Whole steps descending chromatically in 16th note triplets

153: Augmented scale arpeggio pattern, descending

154: Augmented scale arpeggio pattern ascending

155: Whole tone scale with 16th note triplets, ascending

156: Chromatic embellishment on major descending in major 3rds

157: Whole steps in 4ths, descending in half steps

158: Intervallic study in major 3rds separated by 4ths (symmetric augmented)

159: Intervallic study in major 3rds separated by minor 2nds (symmetric augmented)

160: Intervallic study in minor 3rds with neighbor notes, descending in major 3rds (symmetric augmented)

161: Major thirds with chromatic embellishment, ascending and descending in minor 3rds

162: Four-note groups in whole tones, ascending and descending in minor 3rds

163: Two augmented triads a minor 3rd apart, in all inversions (Symmetric augmented) (Gary Campbell)

164: Major 3rds with neighbor, descending in whole steps (whole tone study)
165: First three notes of minor scales in major thirds (Michael Brecker)
166: Augmented triads with neighbor note, ascending and descending in major 3rds
167: Major 3rds with neighbor notes., ascending in minor 3rds
168: Intervallic pattern in major 3rds, ascending and descending (Permutation of whole tone scale)
169: Whole tone permutation, ascending and descending in major 3rds
170: Intervallic permutation: 4ths with neighbor notes, ascending in major 3rds
171: Intervallic permutation: "4th up 5th down", descending in major 3rds
172: Pairs of 4ths a half step apart, ascending in whole steps
173: The inverse of #172
174: Permutation of V 7+5, ascending chromatically
175: Augmented scale fragments descending in whole tones
176: The inverse of #175
177: Ascending augmented scale fragments ascending chromatically
178: Descending augmented scale fragments, ascending chromatically
179: Descending augmented scales, ascending in minor 3rds
180: Descending augmented scales, descending in minor 3rds
181: Augmented scale permutation in tritones, ascending chromatically
182: Augmented scales, one up one down, (minor 3rd to half step) ascending chromatically, using common tone
183: Augmented triads with upper neighbors, ascending chromatically (augmented scale permutation)
184: Augmented scale fragments in tritones, descending in whole steps
185: "The other side" of #182 (Half step followed by minor 3rd)
186: Descending 5ths with neighbor note, ascending in whole steps
187: Minor 6th to tritone with neighbor note, ascending in whole steps

Section 3: Diminished/Minor 3rds. 41

188: Diminished triads in whole steps ascending & descending on II V I
189: Chromatic minor third pattern (Phil Woods)
190: Chromatic minor 3rd pattern ascending chromatically
191: Chromatic ascending minor third pattern (Phil Woods)
192: Diminished pattern with passing tones
193: Chromatic minor 3rd ascending pattern
194: Intervallic pattern, minor 3rds with double chromatic approach, ascending in half steps
195: Minor third and three chromatic notes, ascending in half steps
196: Whole steps ascending in minor 3rds with 16th triplet embellishment (Diminished scale permutation)
197: Same as #196 but descending
198: Four diminished triads ascending in whole steps on V7 to I
199: Minor thirds, one up, one down, in four-note groups, ascending in minor thirds. (Diminished pattern)
200: Minor thirds, one up, one down, in four-note groups of whole steps, descending in minor thirds
201: Chromatic intervallic pattern descending in minor thirds
202: Minor thirds with chromatic neighbor notes, ascending chromatically

203: A diminished scale pattern (Stan Getz, Sonny Stitt)
204: Same as # 203, descending
205: A diminished scale pattern based on #203
206: Same pattern as #205, ascending in half steps
207: Minor 3rds in 16th note triplets, ascending chromatically
208: Chromatic/Diminished scale hybrid (Barry Harris)
209: Same as #179 in ascending form
210: Same as #179: chromatic/diminished scale hybrid (Barry Harris) ascending in minor 3rds
211: Minor 3rd pattern ascending in minor 3rds
212: Minor 3rd pattern descending in minor 3rds
213: Minor 7ths ascending and descending in minor 3rds
214: Two diminished scale fragments a tritone apart
215: Series of chromatic triplets ascending in minor thirds
216: Chromatic triplets separated by a tritone, descending in minor 3rds
217: Chromatic triplets separated by a tritone, ascending in minor 3rds
218: Ascending diminished triads with lower chromatic neighbor, ascending in minor 3rds ("Diminished Pyramids")
219: "Diminished Pyramids" descending in minor 3rds
220: Descending diminished triads with upper chromatic neighbor note, ascending chromatically
221: Same as #220, descending chromatically
222: Two diminished scale permutations, separated by half steps, descending in minor 3rds
223: Four ascending chromatics and tritone, ascending in minor 3rds (diminished permutation)
224: Same as #223, descending in minor 3rds
225: Four descending chromatics and tritone, ascending in minor 3rds
226: Same as #225, but descending in minor 3rds
227: Diminished permutation with chromatics: four up - three down, ascending in minor 3rds
228: Minor 3rds with neighbor, descending in whole steps (Dizzy Gillespie)
229: Minor thirds with chromatic neighbor, ascending in whole steps
230: Four ascending chromatics into four descending notes of diminished scale, ascending in minor 3rds
231: Minor 3rds with neighbor notes, separated by a descending tritone, descending chromatically
232: Minor 3rds with chromatic neighbors on diminished 7th chords, ascending in half steps
233: Perfect 5ths with neighbor notes, ascending in minor 3rds
234: Chromatic approach to diminished arpeggio
235: Diminished 7th arpeggios with chromatic neighbor note, one up, one down, ascending chromatically
236: Descending diminished 7th arpeggios with neighbor notes, ascending chromatically
237: Intervallic permutation of diminished triad with neighbor note on bottom and 4th on top, ascending in minor 3rds
238: Same as #368 (172), descending in minor thirds
239: Minor 3rds with neighbor notes, one up one down
240: Minor 3rds with neighbor notes, ascending in whole steps
241: Minor 3rd and 4th with neighbor notes, ascending chromatically
242: Minor 3rd to half step up and down, moving in 4ths
243: Major 7ths with 16th note triplets and chromatic neighbors, ascending in minor 3rds
244: Ascending tritones with lower chromatic neighbors, ascending in minor 3rds

Section 4: Cyclic/Progressions 52

- 245: Pattern in 4ths resolving to major
- 246: Diatonic II V I phrase with neighbor notes in cycle
- 247: Minor 9th Arpeggios in minor thirds over II V I
- 248: Ascending & descending chords on II- flat II - I
- 249: same as #248 but all descending
- 250: Same as #248 but all ascending
- 251: Same as #248 but reverse directions
- 252: 8th note bebop phrase (Bud Powell)
- 253: Ascending minor 3rds with chromatic neighbors, moving in cycle
- 254: Charlie Parker "Red Cross"
- 255: Dominant pattern V I major and minor
- 256: II7 V7 I major, using diminished
- 257: II V I phrase with suspended resolution
- 258: 13th chords with flatted 9th, moving in cycle
- 259: Harmonic shift from II-7 to IV -7 as a substitute for II V I
- 260: Use of "Altered Upper Structure"
- 261: Minor triads a tritone apart, used on II V I
- 262: V7 to I using altered upper structure
- 263: A 16th triplet neighbor-note pattern on a V I, moving in the cycle of 5ths
- 264: Four Minor to Flat-Seven Seventh, resolving to the tonic, moving in cycle of 5ths
- 265: IV-7 or flat II to I
- 266: Chromatic approach to the 3rd skipping to the 9th on a minor 7th chord, in a 2 : 3 rhythmic feel
- 267: Symmetrical phrase using tritone substitution
- 268: Chromatic "passageway" connecting the 7th of II-7 to the 7th of V7
- 269: "Chromatic passageway" leading to melodic minor "spiral" on tritone, to "spiral" on I major
- 270: Parallel phrases in tritones on a II V I
- 271: Approaches to II flat II I using upper structures. (Jimmy Raney)
- 272: III flat III II flat II I using arpeggiated chords with chromatic embellishment (Charlie Parker)
- 273: II V I phrase with chromatic embellishments, ascending in minor thirds
- 274: V7alt to I major lydian phrase, ascending chromatically
- 275: 7th to 3rd phrase on II V's, ascending chromatically
- 276: Quarter note phrase on IV minor or flat II progression (Freddie Redd)
- 277: Minor 9th arpeggios a tritone apart played in triplets over II V I
- 278: II V I phrase using minor triads a tritone apart
- 279: Diminished scale permutation on V7 to I, descending chromatically
- 280: Stacked 4ths over V7 to I, ascending in minor 3rds
- 281: II V I phrase using stacked 4ths a half step apart, descending chromatically
- 282: Arpeggios using tritone substitution
- 283: "Chromatic Spirals" a tritone apart over II flat II I
- 284: Descending Dorian mode parallel phrases a tritone apart, over II V I
- 285: Stacked 4ths pattern with chromatic neighbor notes on II V I, descending in whole steps
- 286: Descending 4ths phrase over a II V I
- 287: "Backcycling" using whole tones built on the third
- 288: Minor 7th arpeggio descending from 7 to 3, a tritone apart (Sonny Rollins)

289: Melodic Minor scale fragment with chromatic neighbor notes, resolving to the 3rd of I major, moving in cycle of 5ths
290: Permutations of minor 7th arpeggios separated by minor 3rds, over II V I
291: Dominant arpeggios from 3 to 9, separated by minor 3rds, resolving to I major 9 (minor 3rd pyramid)
292: Upper structure melodic minor arpeggio, in tritones, over II V I
293: "Back Door", moving in cycle of 5ths
294: Diminished permutation on V7 to I
295: V7 to I using diminished 7th arpeggio, resolving to major triad, and major 7th
296: Upper structure pattern on dominant 7th chords using #11 and 13 (Tadd Dameron)
297: Diatonic 6ths with chromatic embellishment, moving cyclically over II V I
298: tritone key II V resolution to major (Kenny Dorham)
299: Parallel phrases a tritone apart used on II V I
300: Minor 7th to diminished arpeggios on a II V I
301: Diatonic 3rds into diminished triad with neighbor notes, resolving to major ("Diminished Sandwiches")
302: Major scale permutation to ascending diminished 7th chord, resolving to major (in the same key)
303: Same as #220 resolving to major, in cycle of 5ths
304: Dominant 7ths voiced 1 7 5 3 in tritones, resolving to the 3rd of major, moving in cycle of 5ths
305: 7 #9 #11 arpeggios, separated by tritones, resolving to major, moving in cycle of 5ths
306: Diminished triad with a 4th on top, resolving to 3rd of major, ascending chromatically
307: Ascending diatonic arpeggios to descending diminished scale on a II V I, in cycle of 5ths (Hank Jones)
308: "Spiral" on II V I ascending chromatically
309: Major scale permutation to descending diminished 7th chord, resolving to major, descending in whole steps
310: Minor 3rds with neighbor notes, separated by an ascending tritone, moving in cycle of 5ths
311: II V pattern with neighbor notes to 7b5
312: Scale notes on II-7 to chromatics on V7 resolving to I, in cycle of 5ths
313: A variation on #312
314: Tritone key cadence, using 9 11 6 5
315: Minor 3rd, major 3rd to double chromatic, moving in cycle of 5ths
316: Chromatic passageway into melodic minor on II V
317: II V phrase using neighbor note of #11, ascending chromatically
318: 4th pattern on altered II V, ascending chromatically
319: Descending 4th pattern on II V, descending chromatically
320: Arpeggios using major and minor 7ths to tritone key, over II V I
321: Descending permutation pattern on II V
322: Ascending permutation pattern on II V
323: "Chromatic Passageway" from the 3rd to the 7th of dominants, ascending and descending, moving in cycle of 5ths
324: Minor thirds with chromatic neighbor, ascending in whole steps, to descending to diminished 7th arpeggio over II V I
325: Same as #324 but descending over II V , moving down chromatically (Phil Woods)
326: 4ths with neighbor notes descending in whole steps to altered dominant, descending chromatically
327: Major 3rds descending chromatically over II V I, descending chromatically

328: 7th to 3rd movement on II V with neighbor notes, ascending chromatically
329: Diatonically descending in triplets with neighbor notes over II V, descending chromatically (Charlie Parker)
330: Same as #62, but resolving to major in a II V I
331: Dominant 13 #11(or minor) figure, descending chromatically

Section 5: Tritones 71

332: Tritones Ascending in Major 3rds
333: Tritones & Major 3rds permutation: one up one down, resolving to major
334: Triads a tritone apart in all inversions
335: Triads a tritone apart used on II V I
336: Triads a tritone apart alternating while ascending in all inversions
337: Minor triads a tritone apart in close inversions, triplet pattern
338: Whole steps 16th note triplets with tritone, ascending chromatically
339: Intervallic pattern in tritones
340: Inverted arpeggios a tritone apart, over dominant 7th.
341: Major 6th arpeggios spelled 1 5 3 6, separated by a tritone
342: Minor 7th arpeggios spelled 5 1 3 7, separated by tritones
343: Major triads separated by a tritone, ascending in root position, descending in 1st inversion
344: Major triads a tritone apart, descending in alternating inversions
345: Intervallic sequence (three chromatics and a 4th) in tritones, ascending chromatically

Section 6: Dominant 7ths 74

346: Dominant 13th arpeggios a flatted 5th apart used over II V I
347: Mixolydian "Spirals" (Dominant 7th scale with chromatic neighbor notes) descending & ascending
348: Descending third inversion dominant 7th arpeggios, ascending in half steps
349: Descending third inversion dominant 7th arpeggios, descending in half steps
350: Descending third inversion dominant 7th arpeggios in cycle of 5ths
351: Descending 2nd inversion dominant 7th arpeggios, ascending in half steps
352: Same as #351, but descending in half steps
353: Same as #351, but in cycle of 5ths
354: Descending 2nd inversion dominant 7th arpeggios with flat 5 on the bottom, ascending in half steps
355: Same as #354, but descending in half steps
356: Same as #355, but moving in cycle of 5ths
357: Descending 3-note dominant 7th pattern (5 3 7), ascending in half steps
358: Same as #357, but descending in half steps
359: Same as #357, but moving in cycle of 5ths
360: Dominant 7th upper structure arpeggio pattern in cycle of 5ths
361: Dominant 7th (13th to sharp-11th) with neighbor notes moving cyclically
362: Dominant seventh with chromatic embellishment ascending in minor 3rds
363: four-note diatonic pattern on dominant sevenths descending in minor thirds
364: Pattern on dominant 7ths ascending chromatically
365: Intervallic pattern on dominant 13ths, ascending chromatically
366: Dominant 7th phrase with chromatic neighbor notes, descending in whole steps
367: Upper structure arpeggio on dominant 7th (7 to 13), ascending chromatically

368: Dominant 7 flat 5 phrase, ascending chromatically
369: Dominant 13ths with flat 9 ascending chromatically (Tadd Dameron)
370: Dominant chords voiced 7 9 3 13, in minor 3rds, each four-chord group separated by a half step
371: Descending "Diminished Sandwiches"
372: Diminished "sandwiches" coming down a dominant 7th scale resolving to major
373: Dominant 7 b9 #11 13 descending arpeggios, ascending chromatically
374: Same as #373, but ascending arpeggios
375: 7 b9 #11 13 descending arpeggios, ascending in minor 3rds
376: 7 b9 #11 13 descending arpeggios, descending in minor 3rds
377: Four descending chromatics to b9 #9 ascending in minor 3rds
378: Same as #291, descending in minor 3rds
379: Four ascending chromatics to 7 3 9 of dominant, ascending chromatically
380: Four ascending chromatics to 7 #9 b9 , ascending in minor 3rds
381: Dominant 13th chords, ascending chromatically
382: Dominant 7th chords with chromatics to #9 b9, ascending in minor 3rds
383: Descending altered dominant arpeggios, in groups of 5, ascending chromatically
384: The inverse of #342
385: Like #342 and #343, in alternating directions
386: Dominant 13b9 descending in minor 3rds
387: Dominant 13b9, ascending chromatically
388: Descending altered dominant pattern
389: Permutation of dominant 7th chords, ascending chromatically
390: 1st inversion dominant 7th arpeggios with neighbor note, up and down, ascending chromatically
391: V7#9, descending chromatically
392: "Spirals" on dominant 7ths, ascending chromatically

Section 7: Quartals 83
393: Quartal triad triplets, ascending chromatically
394: Descending 4th patterns a tritone apart
395: descending 4ths in 5-note patterns a tritone apart
396: Quartal triad triplets ascending & descending in minor 3rds
397: Quartal triad triplets, ascending in whole steps
398: Ascending 4ths, descending in whole steps
399: Variations on 4ths and 5ths descending in whole steps
400: Quartal triads in minor 3rds, used on V7 to I
401: Quartal triads ascending in whole steps
402: Quartal triads descending in whole steps
403: 4ths (pentatonic) exercise, ascending chromatically
404: Quartal triads, ascending in whole steps
405: Quartal triads, descending in whole steps
406: Groups of five ascending 4ths, ascending chromatically
407: Groups of five descending 4ths, ascending chromatically

Section 1A: Chromatic

#1 Triplets with descending chromatics, moving in 4ths

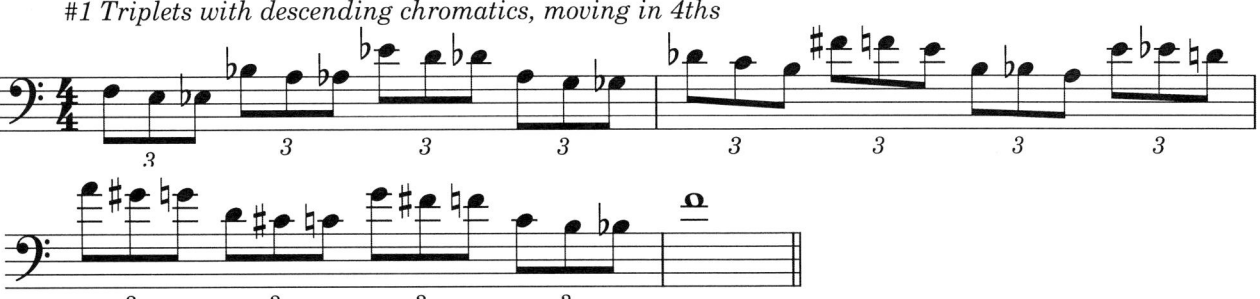

#2 Triplets with descending chromatics in 4ths, used on II V I

#3 as #2 maj 3rd lower

#4 Three chromatics a 4th apart, used over II b II7 I

#5 Chromatic ascending triplets, descending in half steps   *ETC*

THE BOB MOVER JAZZ LEXICON | SECTION 1A: CHROMATIC

#6 Chromatic triplet pattern   ETC

#7 Perfect 5th phrase with chromatic embellishment, ascending chromatically

#8 Intervallic pattern in tritones (#339), but using "Chromatic Passageway"

#9 Chromatic permutation   ETC

#10 Chromatic permutation, ascending in 4ths

#11 Chromatic permutation, descending in 4ths

#12 *4-note chromatic permutation, descending in whole steps*

#13 *A series of four chromatic triplets, each group descending in whole steps (Dizzy Gillespie)*

#14 *Ascending chromatic interval pattern using minor 3rds and tritones*

#15 *Chromatic triplets separated by a tritone, ascending chromatically*

#16 *Chromatic permutation in descending form, ascending and descending in major 3rds*

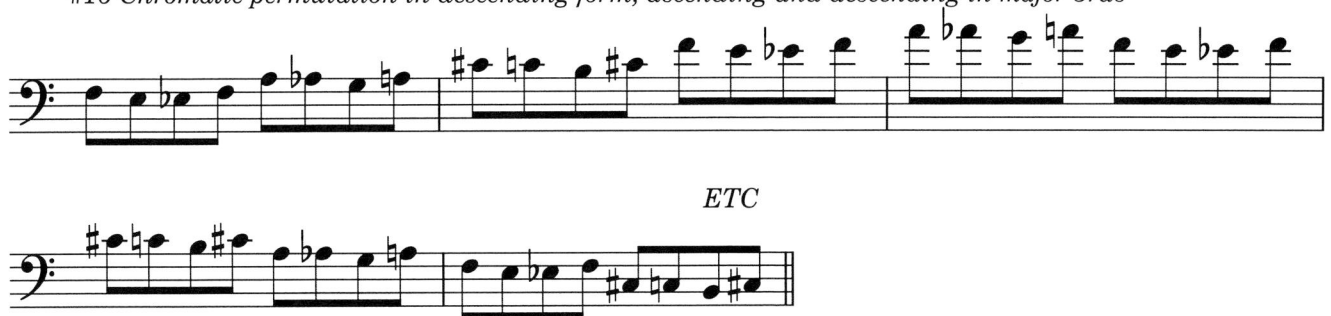

#17 Chromatic permutation in ascending form, ascending and descending in major 3rds

#18 "Chromatic Passageway" in a major 3rd interval, separated and combined, ascending chromatically

#19 Neighbor note enclosures to the 3rd (Dizzy Gillespie), ascending chromatically

#20 Ascending tritone with lower chromatic neighbors, ascending chromatically

#21 Descending tritone with upper chromatic neighbors, ascending chromatically

#22 Descending tritone with lower chromatic neighbors, ascending chromatically

#23 Ascending minor 6th to descending 5th, descending chromatically

Section 1B: Scalic

#24 Dorian with chromatic neighbors on II V ascending in half steps   *ETC*

#25 Same pattern of notes resolving to keys minor 3rds apart

#26 Major scale pattern on 6-5 4-3 9-1 with lower chromatic neighbor notes

#27 Same scale relationships as #26 in ascending pattern

#28 Same scale relationships as #26 in descending pattern

#29 Ascending diatonic triplets in 3rds with chromatic neighbors

#30 Same as #29 but descending

#31 Diatonic scale patterns with diatonic neighbors ascending in minor 3rds over II V I

#32 scale permutation with alternating neighbors in minor 3rds (Back Door)

#33 First three notes of minor scale in triplets, moving in cycle

#34 Diatonic scale pattern on dominant 7ths, descending in half steps

D7   Db7   C7

#35 pentatonic pattern descending in minor thirds

#36 Four-note lick based on dominant or blues scale, ascending in half steps

#37 Diatonic scale permutation descending chromatically

#38 Diatonic 6ths with neighbor notes, descending

#39 1 2 3 5 pattern, descending chromatically

#40 Diatonic descending scale pattern, modulating in descending half steps

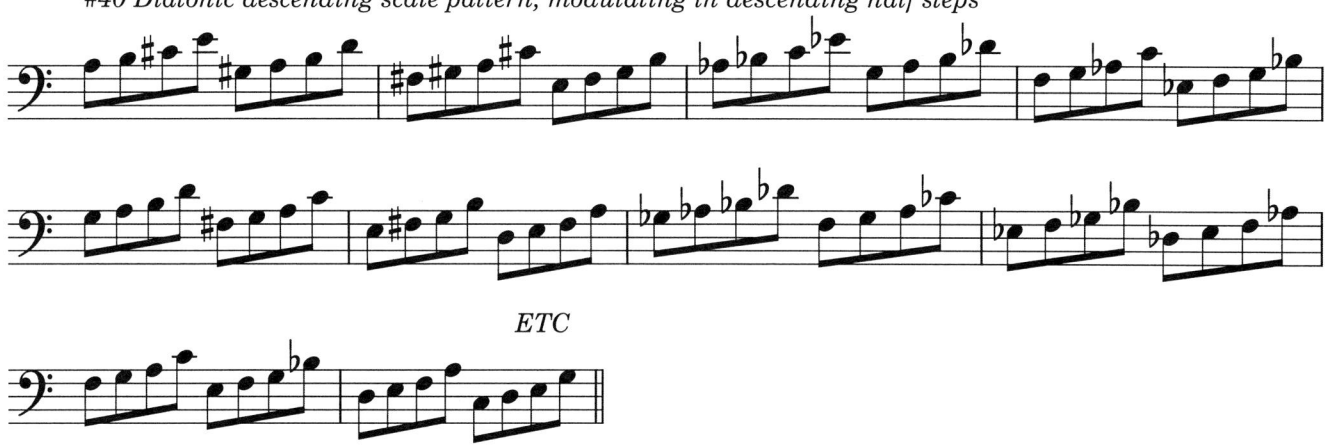

#41 Major 6ths with neighbor notes, descending chromatically

#42 Major 6ths with neighbor notes, ascending chromatically

#43 Diatonic passage with chromatic embellishment, moving in cycle of 5ths   *ETC in all keys*

#44 Major diatonic pattern ascending in whole steps

#45 Major diatonic pattern, one up, one down, ascending in half steps (pentatonic)

#46 Diatonic pattern descending in major thirds

#47 Major to minor phrase using 4ths and 7ths   *ETC in all keys*

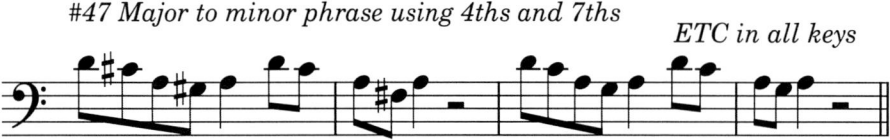

#48 Syncopated phrase ascending chromatically

#49 Minor pentatonic phrase, ascending chromatically   ETC

#50 Bluesy intervallic pattern ascending chromatically   ETC

#51 Pattern of 3 5 2 b2 1, moving in cycle of 5ths.   ETC

#52 Descending chromatic approach to ascending melodic minor scale, in cycle of 5ths

#53 Ascending chromatic approach to descending melodic minor 9th arpeggio, in cycle of 5ths

#54 Minor 6ths with chromatic approach, ascending in whole steps

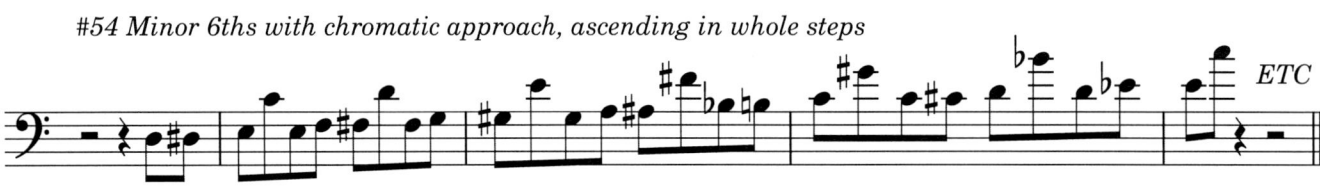

#55 Dorian modes ascending from the 9th to the 9th with chromatic neighbor, and descending arpeggio, 9th to 3

#56 Chromatic "enclosure" of the 3rd of major, ascemnding chromatically

#57 Blues scale phrase, ascending in half steps

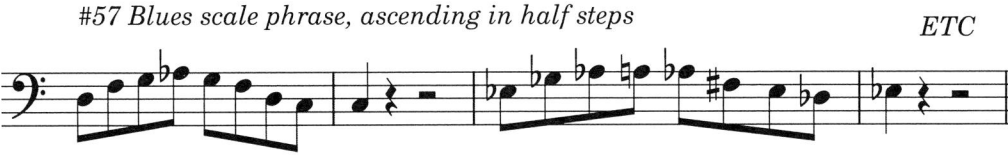

#58 Intervallic study on minor

#59 Intervallic pattern: Descending 4th with chromatic embellishment, ascending chromatically

#60 Inverse of #59

#61 "Spirals" on major, ascending chromatically

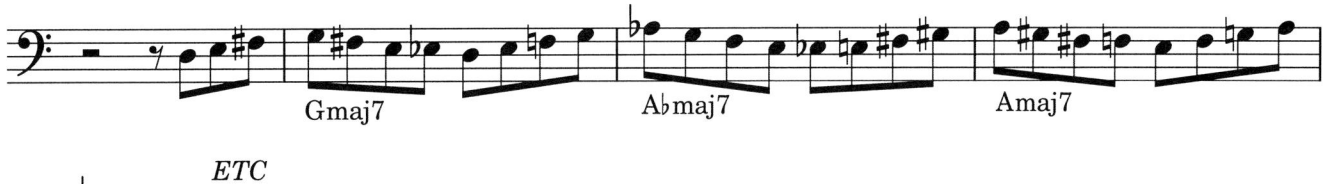

#62 Phrase on melodic minor, descending chromatically

Section 1C: Chords / Arpeggios

#63 Permutation of major 7ths voiced 3 5 7 6, OR minor 7ths voiced 5 7 9 1, descending in minor 3rds

#64 - #63 as used on a II V I

#65 Dorian with chromatic neighbor followed by minor seventh arpeggio ascending chromatically

#66 Minor 7th arpeggios with chromatic neighbor, moving through cycle

#67 Minor 7th arpeggios with chromatic neighbor ascending in minor 3rds

#68 Same as #67 but descending in minor 3rds

#69 same as #67 but ascending in whole tones   ETC

#70 Minor 7th arpeggios with chromatic neighbor a tritone apart used on II V I

#71 Minor 7th arpeggios (ascending form) on II-7 to IV-7 ("Back Door"), resolving to I Lydian

#72 I major and bVII major triads alternating while ascending in all inversions

#73 Diatonic triads descending form with lower chromatic neighbor, ascending the scale

#74 Diatonic triads descending form with lower chromatic neighbor, descending the scale

#75 A diatonic pattern (3 5 2 1) descending in minor 3rds

#76 Minor triads with 9th ascending in half steps

#77 9th chord arpeggios ascending in minor 3rds

#78 same as #77 but one up, one down

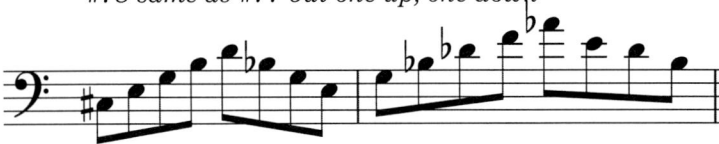

#79 Major triads ascending chromatically alternating root position & 3rd inversion (Lester Young)

#80 Descending second inversion major triads with b5 on the bottom, ascending in half steps

#81 as #80 but descending in half steps

#82 as #80 in cycle of 5ths

#83 Arpeggiated phrase with chromatic neighbor notes, ascending chromatically

#84 Chromatic embellishment on major, moving in cycle of 5ths

#85 An inverted major arpeggio pattern ascending in whole steps

#86 Triadic patterns moving up keys in whole steps (Lee Konitz)

#87 Major triads in second inversion with chromatic neighbors, ascending in half steps

#88 Major triads in root position with lower chromatic neighbor, ascending in whole steps

#89 Two major triads a half step apart with lower chomatic neighbor, alternating inversions

#90 Major triads in second inversion, ascending chromatically

#91 Root position triads with upper chromatic neighbor, ascending in half steps

#92 Minor triads with chromatic neighbor notes ascending in minor thirds

#93 Descending minor triad with upper chromatic neighbor, ascending in minor thirds

#94 Lower chromatic neighbor to the 3rd outlining a major chord, ascending chromatically

#95 Minor 9ths voiced 3 7 3 9, descending in whole steps

#96 Major arpeggio with chromatic neighbor note, ascending in whole steps

#97 Minor triads with neighbor notes, ascending in whole steps

#98 Minor triads with neighbor notes, descending chromatically

#99 Dominant 13th b9 , descending chromatically   ETC

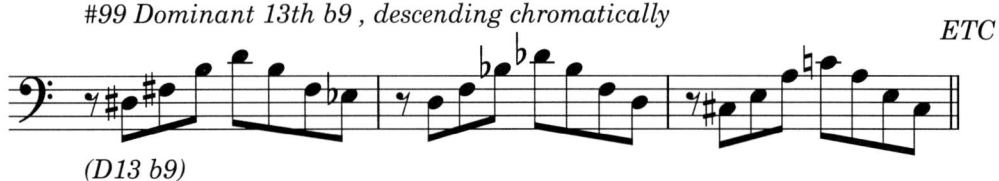

(D13 b9)

#100 Major 9th chords (also could be minor pentatonic), ascending chromatically   ETC

3 5 6 7 9

#101 Same as #100, but in inverse   ETC

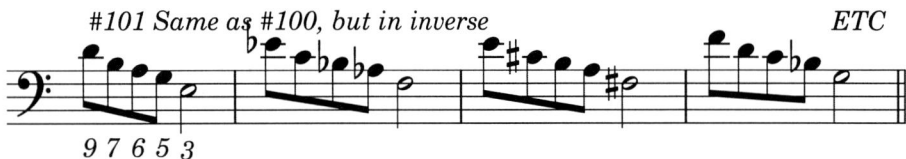

9 7 6 5 3

#102 Major 7ths, voiced 9 1 3 7, ascending chromatically   ETC

9 1 3 7

#103 Same as #102, ascending in minor 3rds

#104 Same as #102, descending in minor 3rds

#105 Minor 7th chords, with "chromatic passageway", descending in minor 3rds

#106 Major 7th arpeggios with neighbor notes, ascending in major 3rds

#107 Intervallic triad pattern, descending in whole steps

#108 Same as #107, ascending in whole steps

#109 A variation on #107, alternating whole steps and tritones

#110 Another intervallic triad pattern, descending in whole steps

#111 1st inversion minor triads with lower chromatic neighbor, ascending chromatically

#112 2nd inversion minor triads with lower chromatic neighbor, ascending chromatically

#113 Root position minor triads with lower chromatic neighbor, ascending chromatically

#114 Same as #113, ascending in whole steps

#115 2nd inversion minor triads with lower chromatic neighbor, descending in whole steps

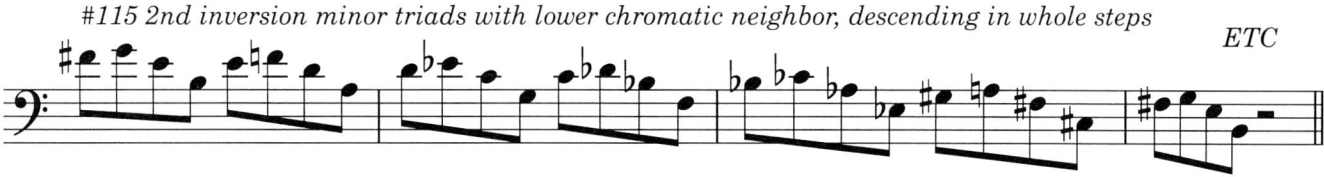

#116 Major 9th chords voiced 5 3 9 7, ascending chromatically

#117 Same as #116 adding chromatic approach

#118 Descending major 6th arpeggios, ascending in minor 3rds

#119 Same as #118, descending in minor 3rds

#120 Descending 2nd inversion minor 7th arpeggios, descending chromatically

#121 Descending major 9th arpeggios, voiced 5 3 9 maj7, ascending in minor 3rds

#122 Same as #121, descending in minor 3rds

#123 1st inversion major triads ascending in major 3rds (symmetric augmented)

#124 1st inversion major triads with lower chromatic neighbor, descending in major 3rds

#125 2nd inversion major triads with lower chromatic neighbor, ascending in major 3rds (symmetric augmented)

#126 An arpeggiated -maj7 chord broken into 7ths, spelling 1 7 3 9 11 6, ascending chromatically
(Yusef Lateef)

#127 Minor 9th with chromatics pattern, ascending in whole steps

#128 Minor triads ascending in major 3rds

#129 Major triads with added 9ths, ascending and descending in major 3rds

#130 Open 5ths with chromatic neighbors in dotted rhythm, ascending chromatically
(Hank Mobley, Charlie Parker)

#131 Minor 7th arpeggios voiced 7 5 1 3, ascending chromatically

#132 Minor 7th arpeggios voiced 9 1 5 7, descending chromatically

#133 Arpeggio pattern on V13b9 (Jackie McLean)

#134 Pattern of 7th to 3rd of II V, ascending in minor 3rds
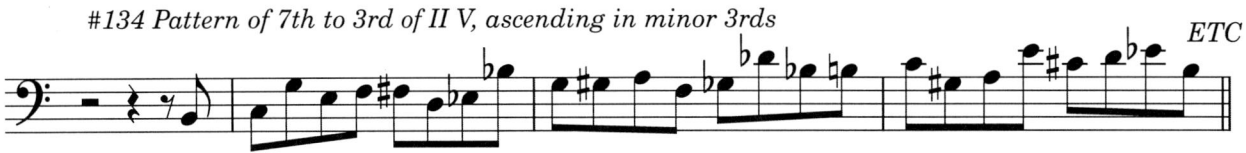

#135 Same as #134, descending in minor 3rds

#136 Permutation of minor 7th chords, ascending chromatically
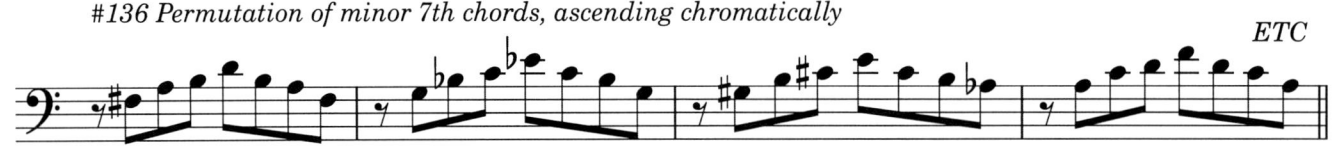

#137 Descending 2nd inversion minor triads, with neighbor notes and 16th note triplets, ascending in whole steps
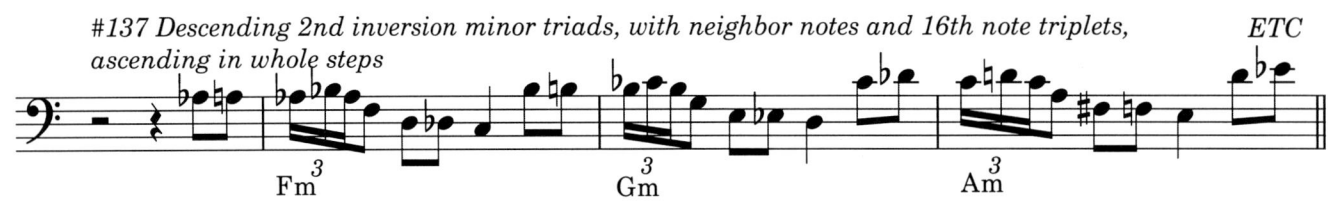

#138 *Descending 2nd inversion major triads, with neighbor notes and 16th note triplets, descending in whole steps*

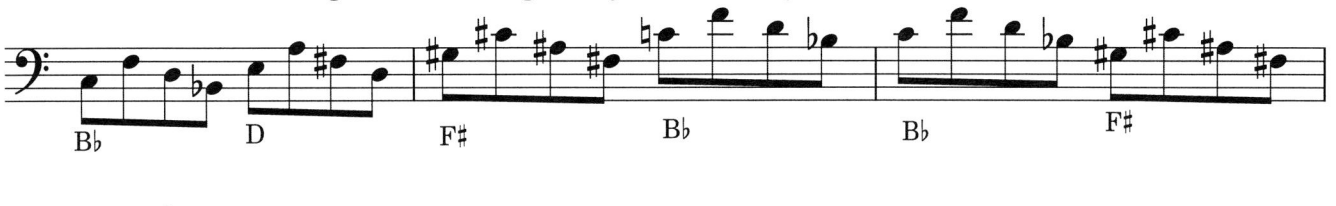

#139 *2 5 3 1 ascending and descending in major 3rds (Sonny Rollins)*

Section 2: Whole Tone / Augmented / Major 3rds

#140 Permutation of augmented scale

#141 Permutation of augmented scale with neighbor notes

#142 Permutation of augmented scale, one down, one up

#143 Augmented triad permutation (1 3 +5 3) ascending in minor 3rds

#144 Augmented triad permutation (3 1 3 +5) ascending in minor 3rds

#145 Whole Tone pattern in major thirds (Bud Powell)

#146 Augmented triads ascending in minor 3rds

#147 parallel major 3rds (John Coltrane)*

Bmaj7   D7   Gmaj7   Bb7   Ebmaj7   F#7   Bmaj7

*Michael Brecker and I used to practice the Slonimsky book together extensively. He found the page which clearly outlined "Giant Steps" and we were both convinced it must have been where Coltrane. drew his inpiration in addition to "Miss Jones"

-Bob

#148 whole steps descending in half steps

#149 intervallic pattern: major 3rds with double chromatic approach, ascending in half steps

#150 same as #149 but descending in half steps

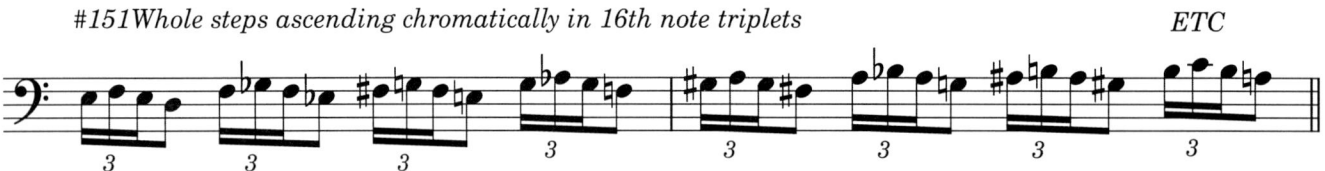

#151 Whole steps ascending chromatically in 16th note triplets

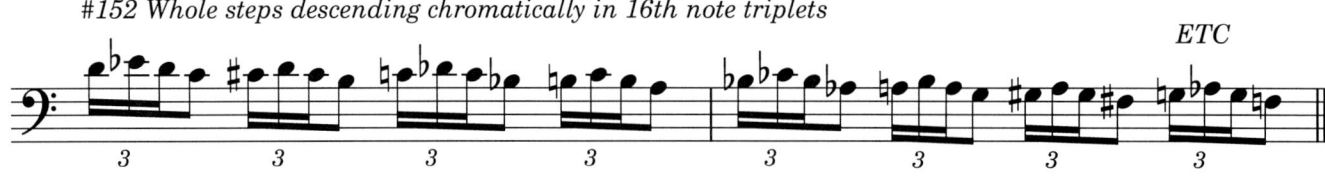

#152 Whole steps descending chromatically in 16th note triplets

#153 Augmented scale arpeggio pattern, descending

#154 Augmented scale arpeggio pattern ascending

#155 Whole tone scale with 16th note triplets, ascending

#156 Chromatic embellishment on major descending in minor 3rds

#157 Whole steps in 4ths, descending in half steps

#158 Intervallic study in major 3rds separated by 4ths (symmetric augmented

#159 Intervallic study in major 3rds separated by minor 2nds (symmetric augmented)

#160 Intervallic study in minor 3rds with neighbor notes, descending in major 3rds (symmetric augmented)

#161 Major thirds with chromatic embellishment, ascending and descending in minor 3rds

#162 Four-note groups in whole tones, ascending and descending in minor 3rds

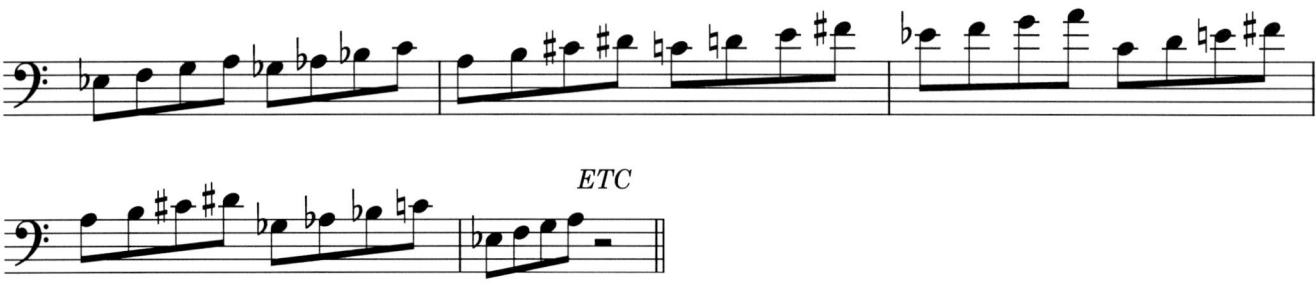

#163 Two augmented triads a minor 3rd apart, in all inversions (Symmetric augmented) (Gary Campbell)

#164 Major 3rds with neighbor, descending in whole steps (whole tone study)

#165 First three notes of minor scales in major thirds (Michael Brecker)

#166 Augmented triads with neighbor note, ascending and descending in major 3rds

#167 Major 3rds with neighbor notes, ascending in minor 3rds

#168 Intervallic pattern in major 3rds, ascending and descending (Permutation of whole tone scale)

#169 Whole tone permutation, ascending and descending in major 3rds

#170 Intervallic permutation: 4ths with neighbor notes, ascending in major 3rds

#171 Intervallic permutation: "4th up 5th down", descending in major 3rds

#172 Pairs of 4ths a half step apart, ascending in whole steps

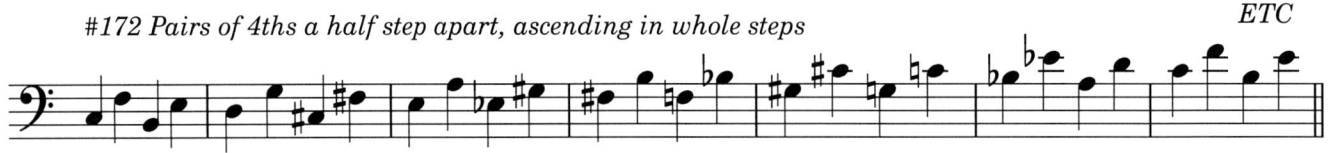

#173 The inverse of #172

#174 Permutation of V 7+5, ascending chromatically

F♯7+5   G7+5   A♭7+5   A7+5

#175 Augmented scale fragments descending in whole tones

#176 The inverse of #175

#177 Ascending augmented scale fragments ascending chromatically

#178 Descending augmented scale fragments, ascending chromatically

#179 Descending augmented scales, ascending in minor 3rds

#180 Descending augmented scales, descending in minor 3rds

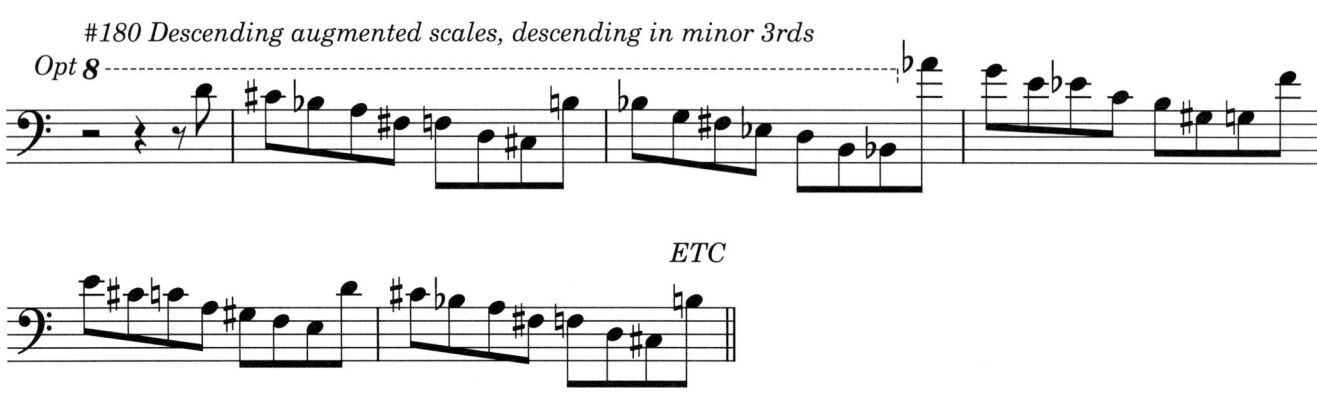

#181 Augmented scale permutation in tritones, ascending chromatically

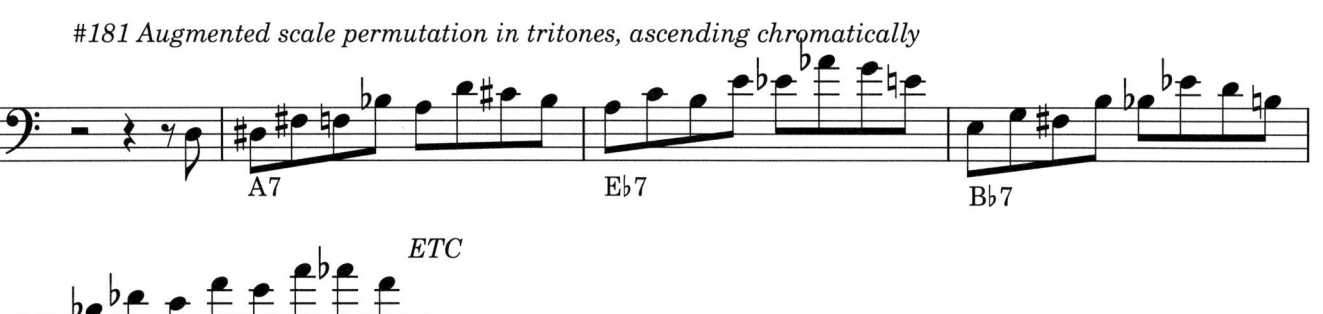

#182 Augmented scales, one up one down, (mior 3rd to half step) ascending chromatically, using common ton

#183 Augmented triads with upper neighbors, ascending chromatically (augmented scale permutation)

#184 Augmented scale fragments in tritones, descending in whole steps

#185 "The other side" of #182 (Half step followed by minor 3rd)

#186 Descending 5ths with neighbor note, ascending in whole steps

#187 Minor 6th to tritone with neighbor note, ascending in whole steps

Section 3: Diminished / Minor 3rds

#188 Diminished triads in whole steps ascending & descending on II V I

#189 Chromatic minor third pattern (Phil Woods)   ETC

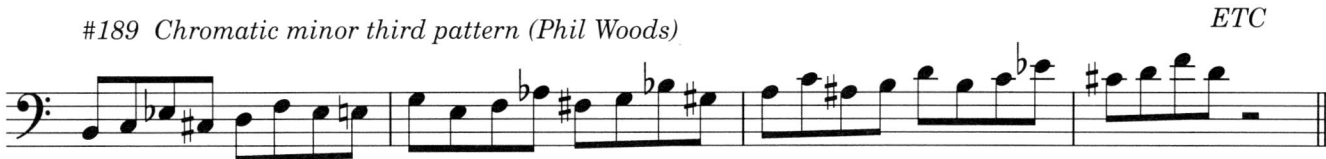

#190 Chromatic minor 3rd pattern ascending chromatically   ETC

#191 Chromatic ascending min3rds (Phil Woods)   ETC

#192 Diminished pattern with passing tones   ETC

#193 Chromatic minor 3rd ascending pattern

#194 Intervallic pattern, minor 3rds with double chromatic approach, ascending in half steps

#195 Minor third and three chromatic notes, ascending in half steps

#196 Whole steps ascending in minor 3rds with 16th triplet embellishment (Diminished scale permutation)

#197 as #196 but descending

#198 Four diminished triads ascending in whole steps on V7 to I

#199 Minor thirds, one up, one down, in four-note groups, ascending in minor thirds. (Diminished pattern)

#200 Minor thirds, one up, one down, in four-note groups of whole steps, descending in minor thirds

#201 Chromatic intervallic pattern ascending in minor thirds

#202 Minor thirds with chromatic neighbor notes, ascending chromatically

#203 A diminished scale pattern (Stan Getz, Sonny Stitt)

#204 Same as #203, descending

#205 A diminished scale pattern based on #203

#206 Same pattern as #205, ascending in half steps

#207 3rds in 16th note triplets, ascending chromatically

#208 Chromatic/Diminished scale hybrid (Barry Harris)

#209 Same as #208 in ascending form

#210 Same as #208: chromatic/diminished scale hybrid (Barry Harris) ascending in minor 3rds

#211 Minor 3rd pattern ascending in minor 3rds

#212 Minor 3rd pattern descending in minor 3rds

#213 Minor 7ths ascending and descending in minor 3rds

#214 Two diminished scale fragments a tritone apart

#215 Series of chromatic triplets ascending in minor thirds

#216 Chromatic triplets separated by a tritone, descending in minor 3rds

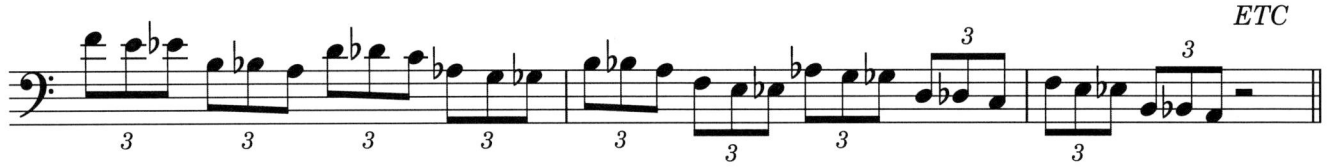

#217 Chromatic triplets separated by a tritone, ascending in minor 3rds

#218 Ascending diminished triads with lower chromatic neighbor, ascending in minor 3rds ("Diminished Pyramids")

#219 "Diminished Pyramids" descending in minor 3rds

#220 Descending diminished triads with upper chromatic neighbor note, ascending chromatically

#221 Same as #220, descending chromatically

#222 Two diminished scale permutations, separated by half steps, descending in minor 3rds

#223 Four ascending chromatics and tritone, ascending in minor 3rds (diminished permutation)

#224 Same as #223, descending in minor 3rds

#225 Four descending chromatics and tritone, ascending in minor 3rds

#226 Same as #225, but descending in minor 3rds

#227 Diminished permutation with chromatics: four up - three down, ascending in minor 3rds

#228 Minor 3rds with neighbor, descending in whole steps (Dizzy Gillespie)

#229 Minor thirds with chromatic neighbor, ascending in whole steps

#230 Four ascending chromatics into four descending notes of diminished scale, ascending in minor 3rds

#231 Minor 3rds with neighbor notes, separated by a descending tritone, descending chromatically

#232 Minor 3rds with chromatic neighbors on diminished 7th chords, ascending in half steps

#233 Perfect 5ths with neighbor notes, ascending in minor 3rds

#234 Chromatic approach to diminished arpeggio
Opt 8va

#235 Diminished 7th arpeggios with chromatic neighbor note, one up, one down, ascending chromatically

#236 Descending diminished 7th arpeggios with neighbor notes, ascending chromatically

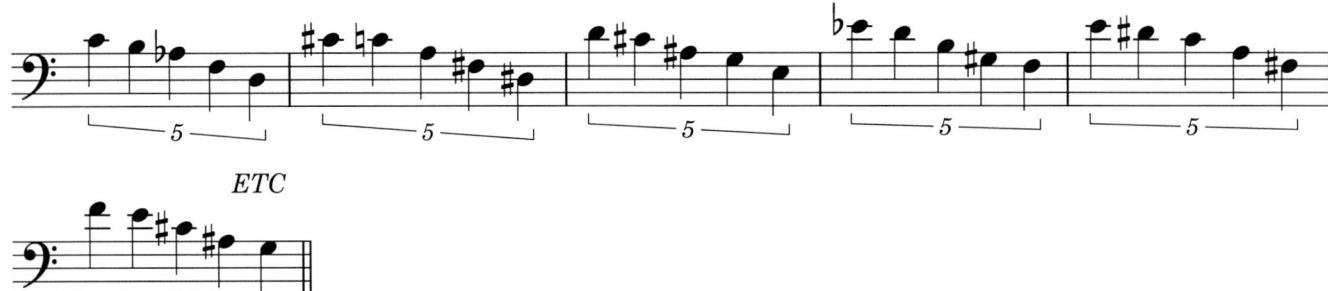

#237 Intervallic permutation of diminished triad with neighbor note on bottom and 4th on top, ascending in minor 3rds

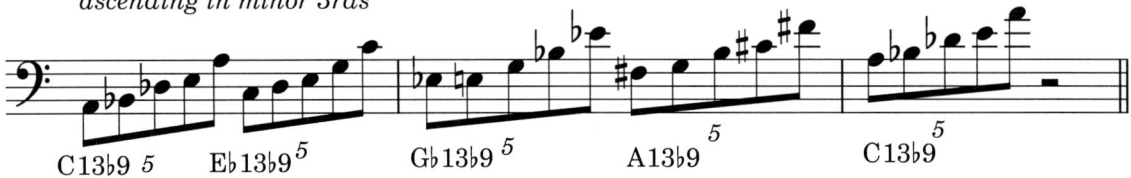

#238 Same as #172, descending in minor thirds

#239 Minor 3rds with neighbor notes, one up one down

#240 Minor 3rds with neighbor notes, ascending in whole steps

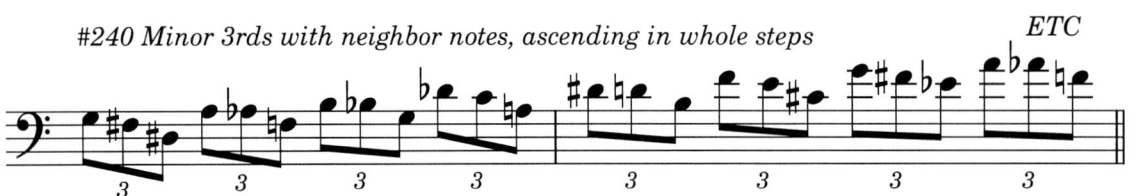

#241 Minor 3rd and 4th with neighbor notes, ascending chromatically

#242 Minor 3rd to half step up and down, moving in 4ths

#243 Major 7ths with 16th note triplets and chromatic neighbors, ascending in minor 3rds

#244 Ascending tritones with lower chromatic neighbors, ascending in minor 3rds

Section 4: Cyclic/Progressions

#245 Pattern in 4ths into bII triad, resolving to 3rd of I major

#246 Diatonic II V I phrase with neighbor notes in cycle

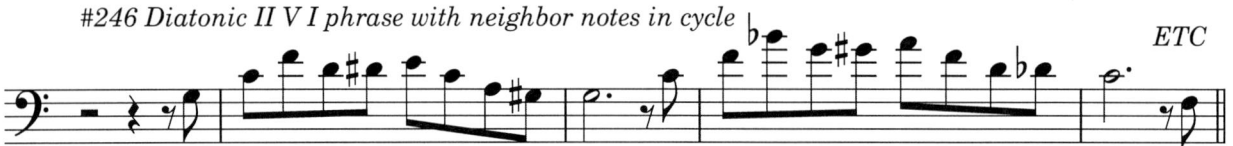

#247 Minor 9th Arpeggios in minor thirds over II V I

Dm7　　　　　　G7alt　　　　　　C

#248 Ascending & descending chords on II - bII - I

#249 same as #248 but all descending

#250 Same as #248 but all ascending

#251 Same as #248 but reverse directions

#252: 8th note bebop phrase on I7 to IV to IV- to I (Bud Powell)

#253 Ascending minor 3rds with chromatic neighbors, moving in cycle

#254 Charlie Parker "Red Cross"

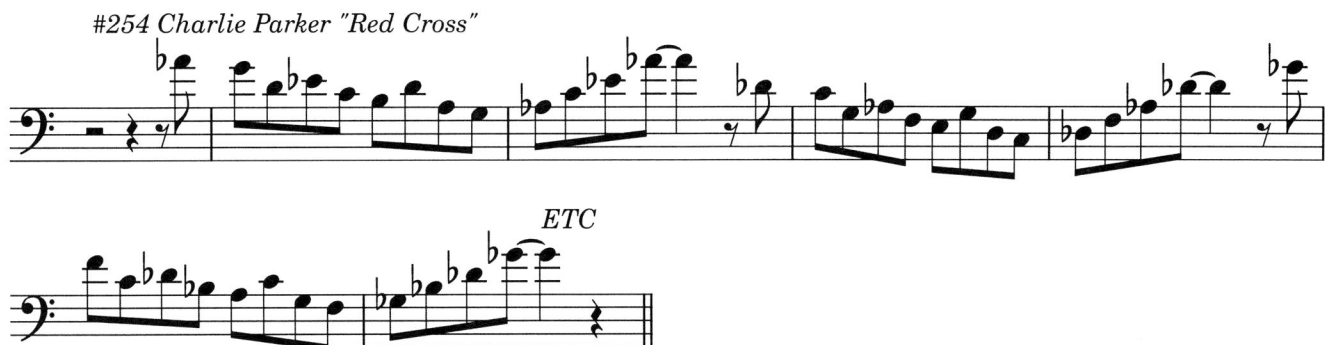

#255 Dominant pattern V I major and minor

#256 II7 V7 I using diminished

#257 II V I phrase with suspended resolution IVminor to I

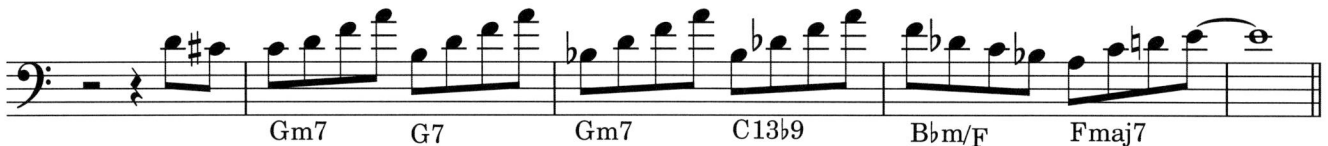

#258 13th chords with flat9 (voiced 7 1 3 13) moving in cycle

#259 Harmonic shift from II -7 to IV-7 as substitute for V7 on a II V I

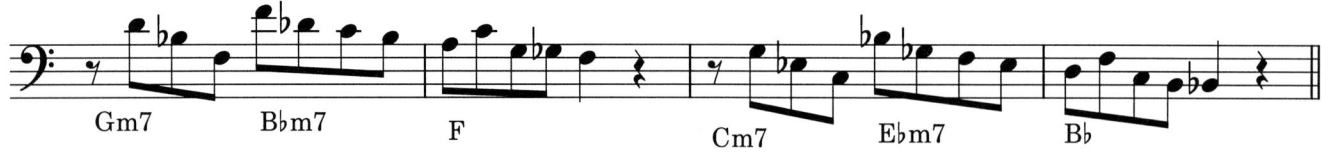

#260 use of altered upper structure b9 #9 b13 on V7 chord in II V I

#261 using minor triads a tritone apart on II V I

#262 V7 to I using altered upper structure

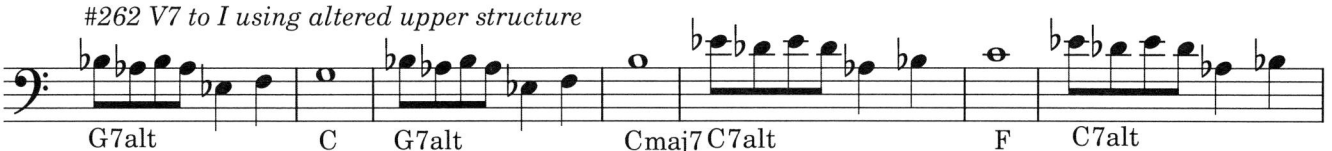

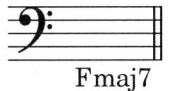

#263 A 16th triplet neighbor-note pattern on a V I, moving in the cycle of 5ths

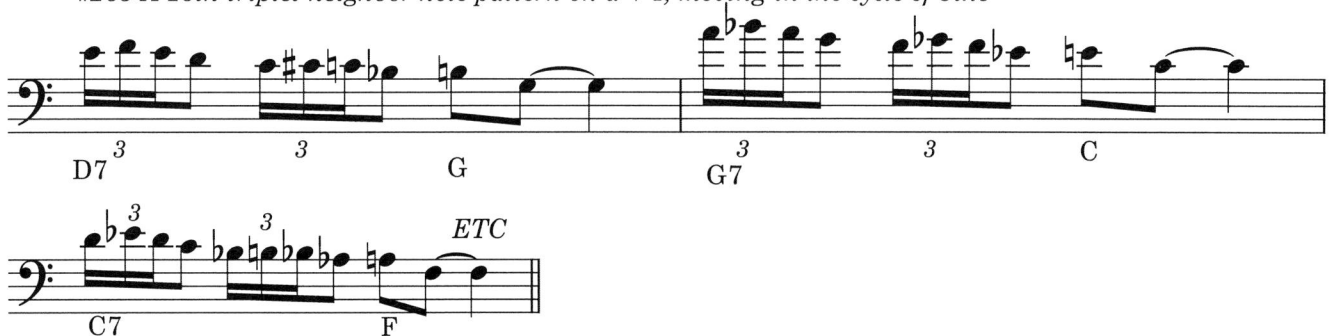

#264 Four Minor to Flat-Seven Seventh, resolving to the tonic, moving in cycle of 5ths

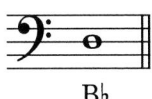

#265 IV-7 to I or bII to I

#266 Chromatic approach to the 3rd skipping to the 9th on a minor 7th chord, in a 2 : 3 rhytmic feel

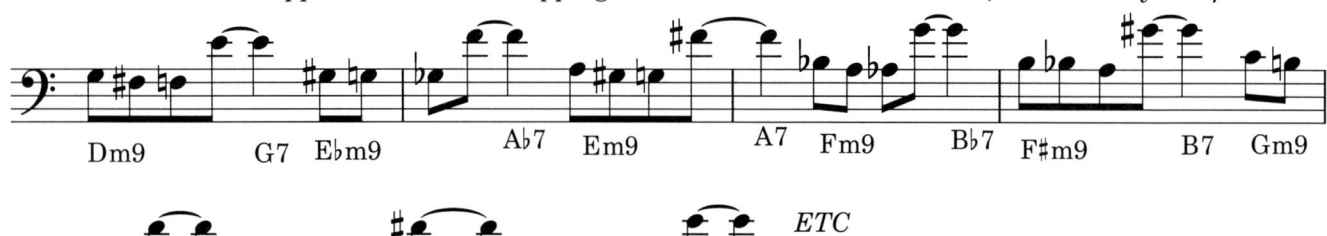

#267 Symmetrical phrase using tritone substitution

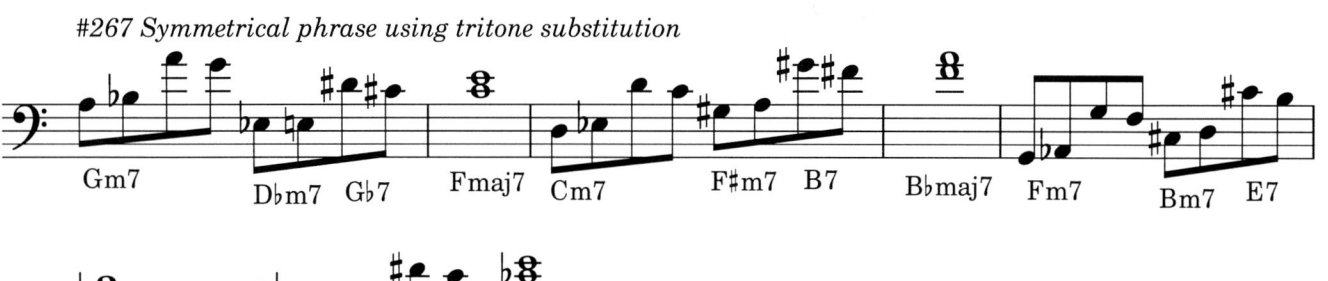

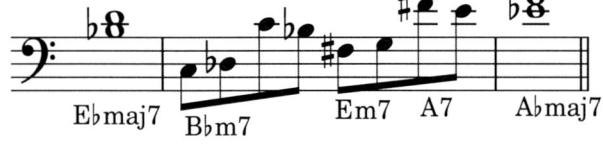

#268 Chromatic "passageway" connecting the 7th of II-7 to the 7th of V7 ascending chromatically

#269 "Chromatic passageway" on II-7 leading to melodic minor "spiral" on tritone, to "spiral" on I major

#270 Parallel phrases in tritones on a II V I

#271 Approaches to II bII I using upper structures. (Jimmy Raney)

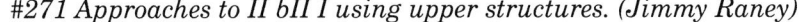

#272 III-7 bIII-7 II-7 bIImaj7 I using arpeggiated chords with chromatic embellishment (Charlie Parker)

#273 II V I phrase with chromatic embellishments, ascending in minor thirds

#274 V7alt to I major lydian phrase, ascending chromatically
(Note: Can also be IVminor or bII7)

#275 7th to 3rd phrase on II V's, ascending chromatically

#276 Quarter note phrase on IVminor or bII7 progression (Freddie Redd)

#277 Minor 9th arpeggios a tritone apart played in triplets over II V I

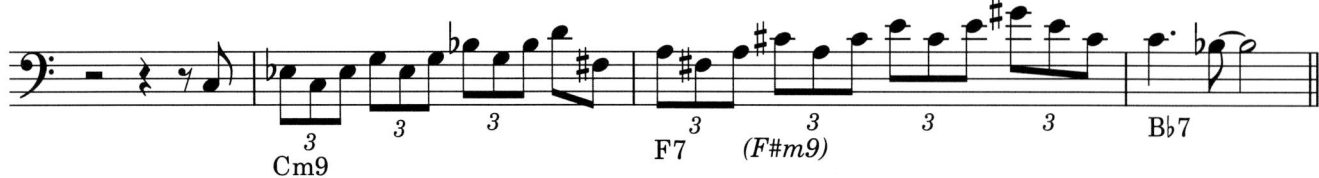

#278 II V I phrase using minor triads a tritone apart

#279 Diminished scale permutation on V7 to I, descending chromatically

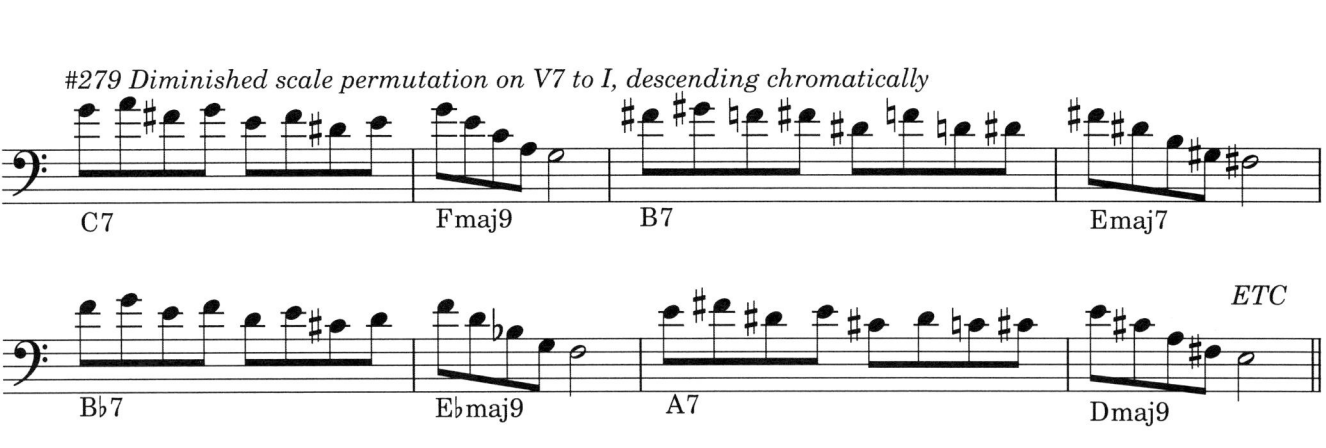

#280 Stacked 4ths over V7 to I, ascending in minor 3rds

#281 II V I phrase using stacked 4ths a half step apart, descending chromatically

#282 Arpeggios using tritone substitution (II-7 bVI-9 bII13 I)

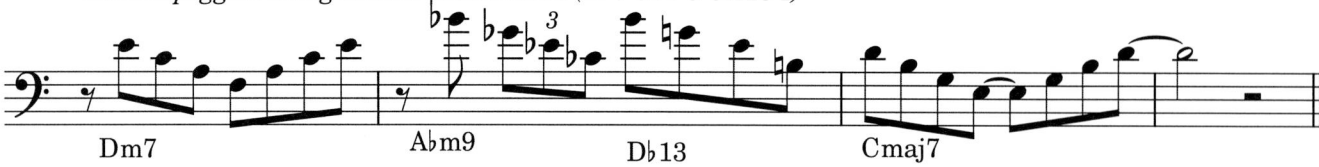

#283 "Chromatic Spirals" a tritone apart over II bII7 I

#284 Descending Dorian mode parallel phrases a tritone apart, over II V I

#285 Stacked 4ths pattern with chromatic neighbor notes on II V I, ascending in half steps

#286 Descending 4ths phrase over a II V I

#287 "Backcycling" from III7 VI7 II7 V7 I using whole tones built on the third

#288 Minor 7th arpeggio descending from 7 to 3, a tritone apart (Sonny Rollins)

#289 Melodic Minor scale fragment with chromatic neighbor notes, resolving to the 3rd of I major, moving in cycle of 5ths

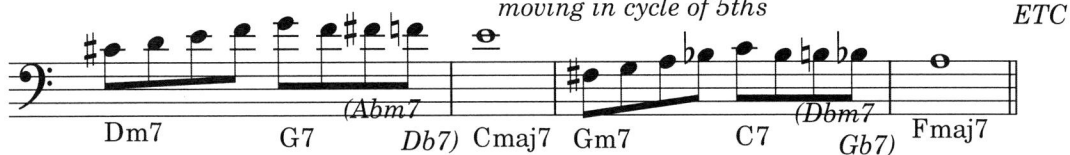

#290 Permutations of minor 7th arpeggios separated by minor 3rds, over II V I

#291 Dominant arpeggios from 3 to 9, separated by minor 3rds, resolving to I major (Minor 3rd "Pyramid")

#292 Upper structure melodic minor arpeggio, in tritones, over II V I

#293 II V I with IV minor as substitute for V7 ("Back Door"), moving in cycle of 5ths

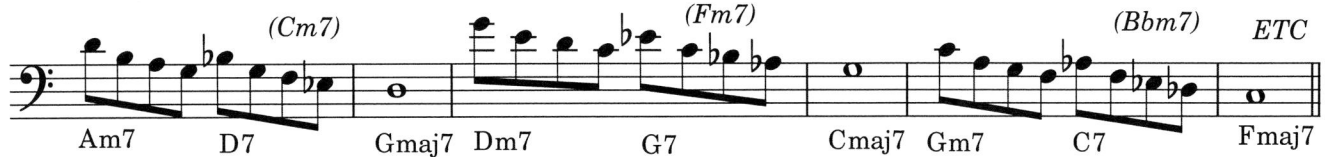

#294 Diminished permutation on V7 to I

#295 V7 to I using diminished 7th arpeggio, resolving to major triad, and major 7th

#296 Upper structure pattern on dominant 7th chords using #11 and 13 in cycle of 5ths (Tadd Dameron)

#297 Diatonic 6ths with chromatic embellishment, moving cyclically over II V I

#298 tritone key II V resolution to major (Kenny Dorham)

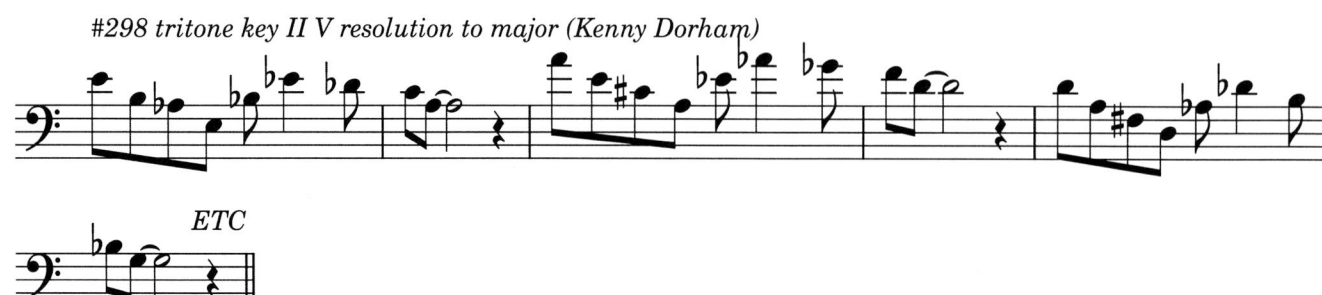

#299 Parallel phrases a tritone apart used on II V I

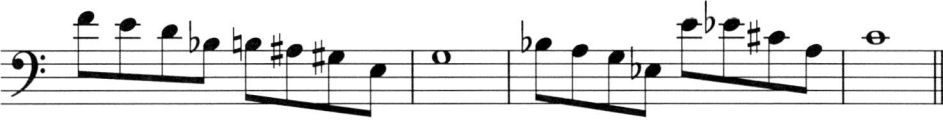

#300 Minor 7th to diminished arpeggios on a II V I

ETC in all keys

#301 Diatonic 3rds into diminished triad with neighbor notes, resolving to major ("Diminished Sandwiches")

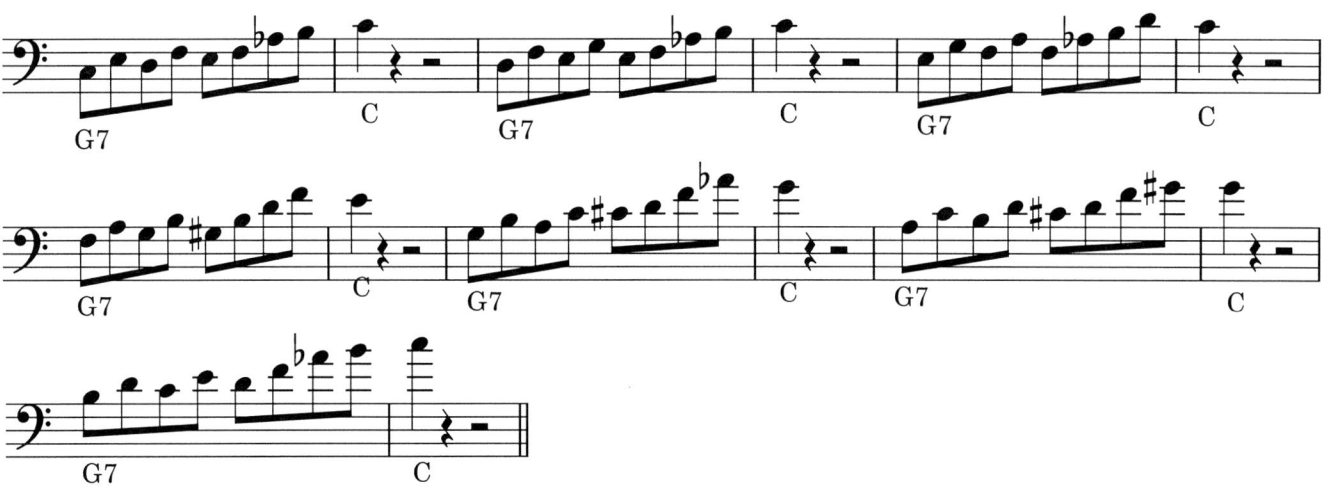

#302 Major scale permutation to ascending diminished 7th chord, resolving to major (in the same key)

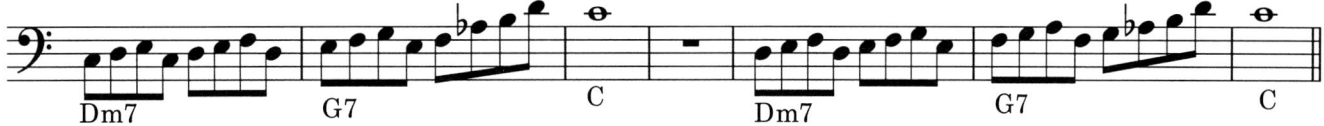

#303 Same as #220 resolving to major, in cycle of 5ths

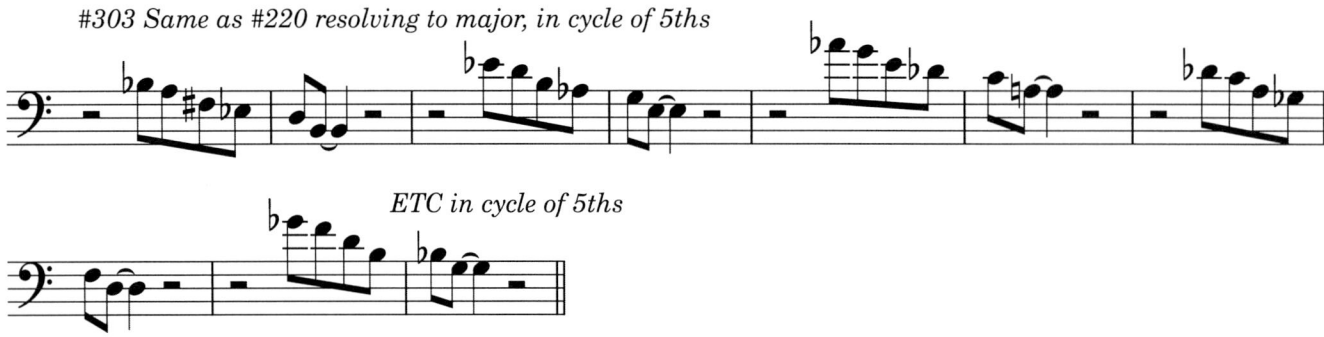

#304 Dominant 7ths voiced 1 7 5 3 in tritones, resolving to the 3rd of major, moving in cycle of 5ths

#305 7 #9 #11 arpeggios, separated by tritones, resolving to major, moving in cycle of 5ths

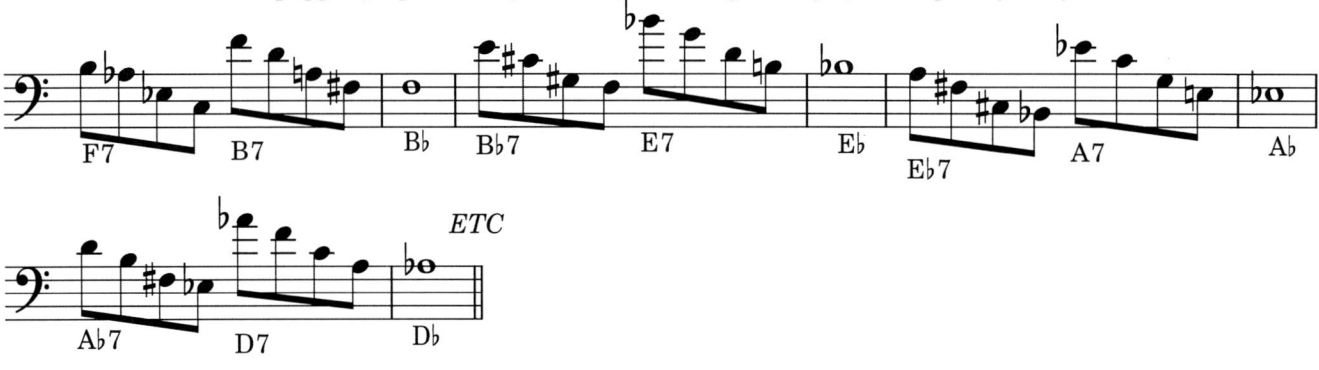

#306 Diminished triad with a 4th on top, resolving to 3rd of major, ascending chromatically

#307 Ascending diatonic arpeggios to descending diminished scale on a II V I, in cycle of 5ths (Hank Jones)

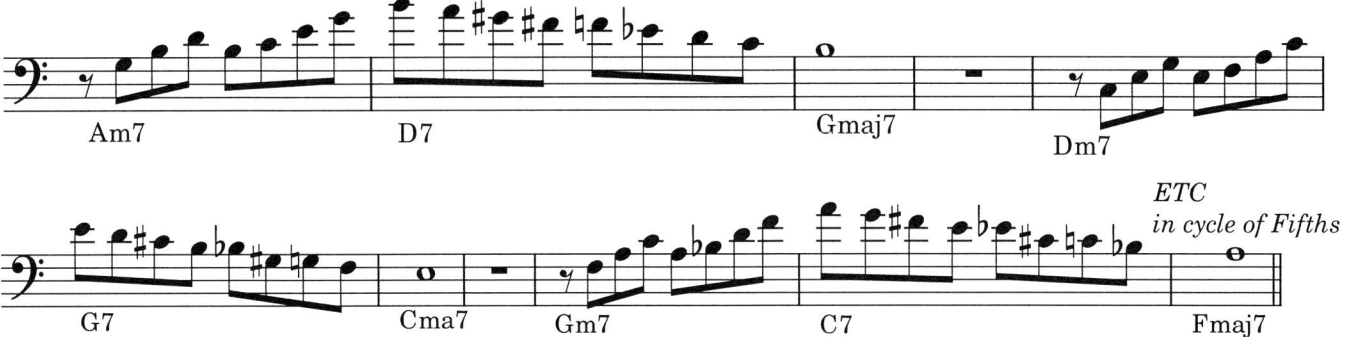

#308 "Spiral" on II V I ascending chromatically

#309 Major scale permutation to descending diminished 7th chord, resolving to major, descending in whole steps

#310 Minor 3rds with neighbor notes, separated by an ascending tritone, moving in cycle of 5ths

#311 II V pattern with neighbor notes to 7b5

#312 Scale notes on II-7 to chromatics on V7 resolving to I , in cycle of 5ths

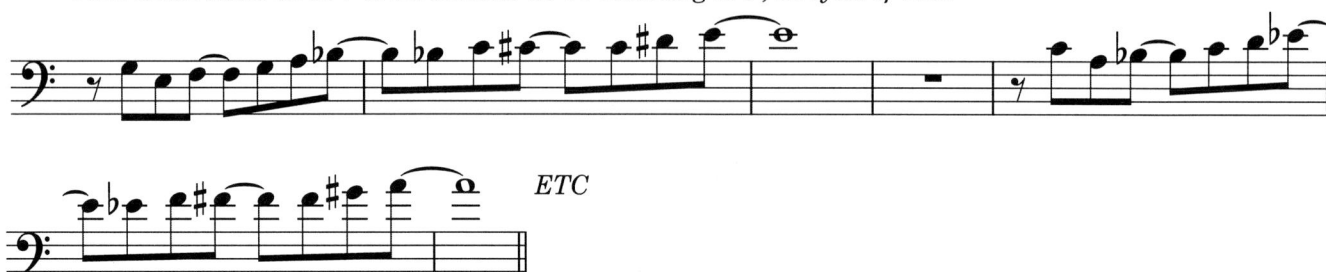

#313 A variation on #312

#314 Tritone key cadence, using 9 11 6 5

#315 Minor 3rd, major 3rd to double chromatic, moving in cycle of 5ths

#316 Chromatic passageway into melodic minor on II V ETC
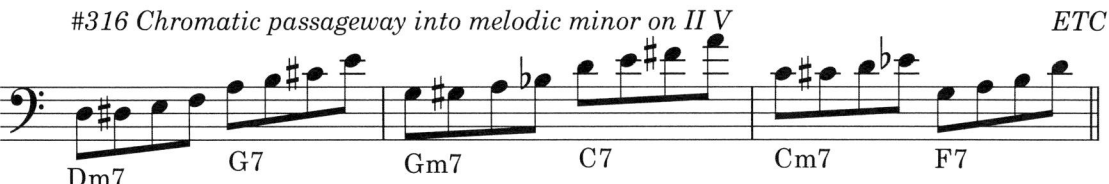

#317 II V phrase using neighbor note of #11. ascending chromatically ETC

#318 4th pattern on altered II V, ascending chromatically
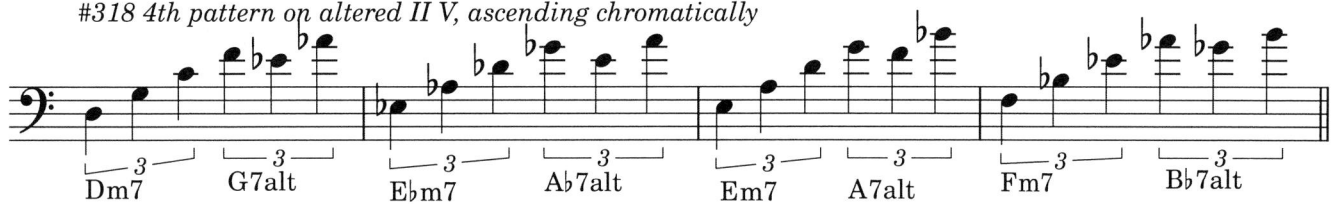

#319 Descending 4th pattern on II V, descending chjromatically ETC
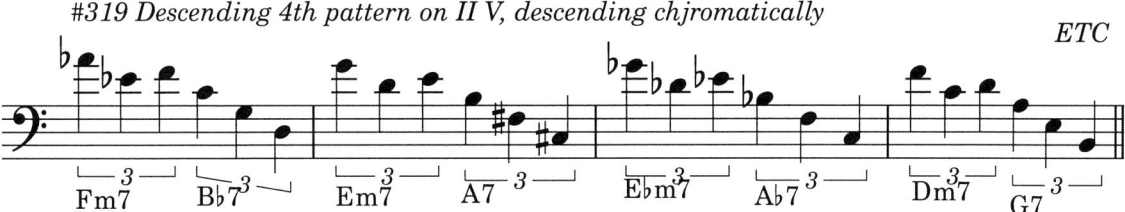

#320 Arpeggios using major and minor 7ths to tritone key, over II V I

#321 Descending permutation pattern on II V

#322 *Ascending permutation pattern on II V*

#323 *"Chromatic Passageway" from the 3rd to the 7th of dominants, ascending and descending, moving in cycle of 5ths*

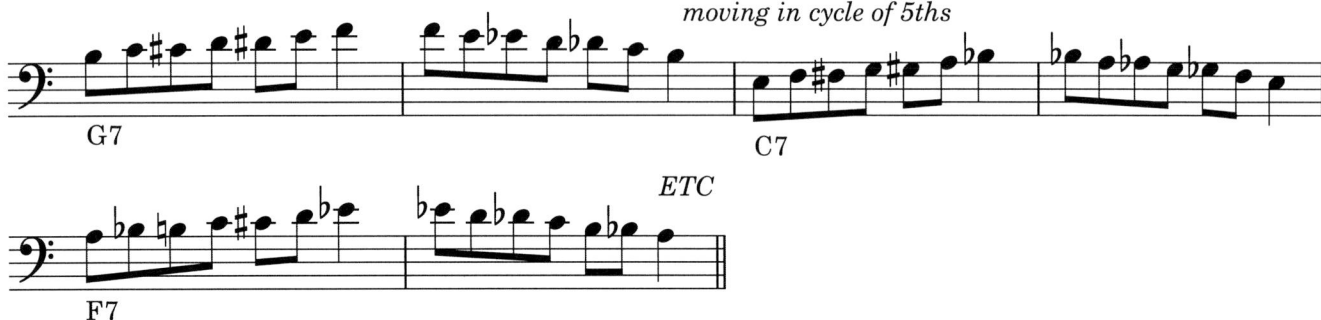

#324 *Minor thirds with chromatic neighbor, ascending in whole steps, to descending to diminished 7th arpeggio over II V I*

#325 *Same as #324 but descending over II V, moving down chromatically (Phil Woods)*

#326 4ths with neighbor notes descending in whole steps to altered dominant, descending chromaticallty

#327 Major 3rds descending chromatically over II V I, descending chromatically

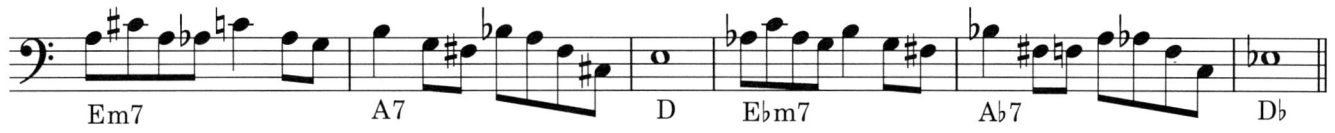

#328 7th to 3rd movement on II V with neighbor notes, ascending chromatically

#329 Diatonically descending in triplets with neighbor notes over II V, descending chromatically (Charlie Parker)

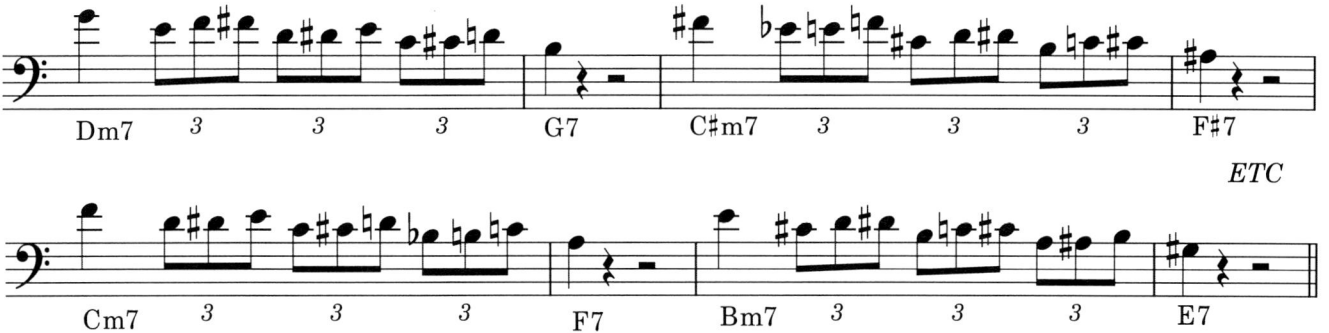

#330 Same as #62, but resolving to major in a II V I   ETC

#331 Dominant 13 #11 (or minor) figure, descending chromatically

Section 5: Tritones

#332 Tritones Ascending in Major 3rds

#333 Tritones & Major 3rds permutation: one up one down, resolving to major

#334 Triads a tritone apart in all inversions

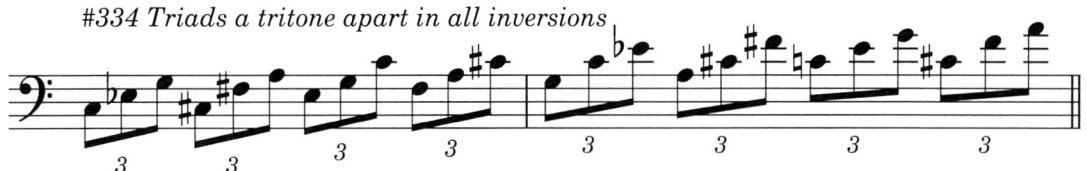

#335 Triads a tritone apart used on II V

#336 Triads a tritone apart alternating while ascending in all inversions

#337 minor triads a tritone apart

#338 Whole steps 16th note triplets with tritone, ascending chromatically

#339 Intervallic pattern in tritones

#340 Inverted arpeggios a tritone apart, over dominant 7th.

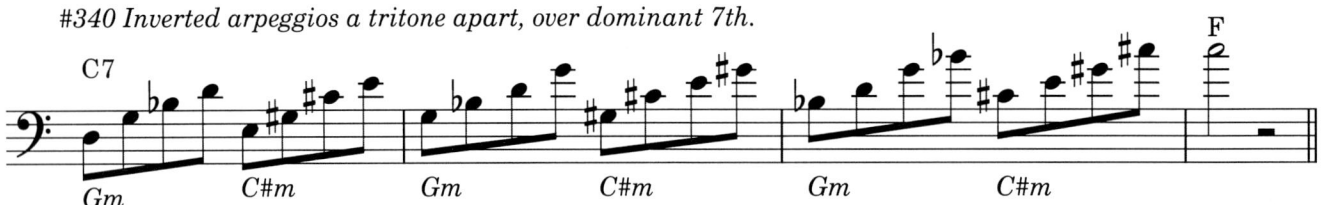

#341 Major 6th arpeggios spelled 1 5 3 6, separated by a tritone

#342 Minor 7th arpeggios spelled 5 1 3 7, separated by tritones

#343 Major triads separated by a tritone, ascending in root position, descemding in 1st inversion

#344 Major triads a tritone apart, descending in alternating inversions

#345 Intervallic sequence (three chromatics and a 4th) in tritones, ascending chromatically

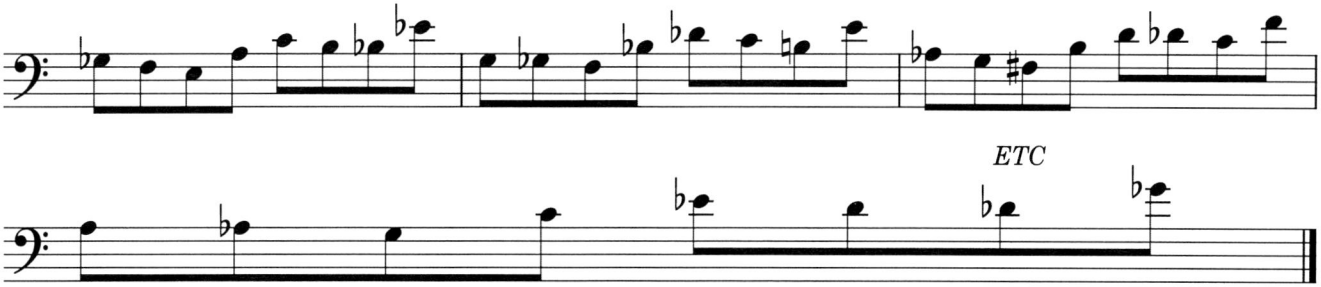

Section 6: Dominant 7ths

#346 Dominant 13th arpeggios a flatted 5th apart used over II V I

#347 Mixolidian "spirals" (Dominant 7th scale with chromatic neighbor notes) descending & ascending

#348 Descending third inversion dominant 7th arpeggios, ascending in half steps

#349 as #348 descending in half steps

#350 as #348 in cycle of 5ths

#351 Descending 2nd inversion dominant 7th arpeggios, ascending in half steps

#352 as #351 descending in half steps

#353 as #351 in cycle of 5ths

#354 Descending 2nd inversion dominant 7th arpeggios with flat 5 on the bottom, ascending in half steps

#355 as #354 descending in half steps

#356 as #354 in cycle of 5ths

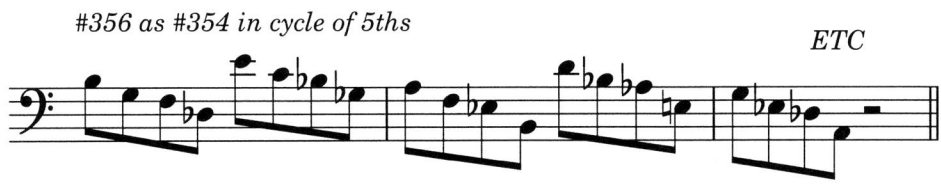

#357 Descending 3-note dominant 7th pattern (5 3 7), ascending in half steps

#358 as #357 descending in half steps   ETC

#359 as #357 in cycle of 5ths   ETC

#360 Dominant 7th upper structure arpeggio pattern in cycle of 5ths   ETC

Eb13   Ab13   Db13

#361 Dominant 7th (13th to sharp-11th) with neighbor notes moving cyclically   ETC

Eb13   Ab13   Db13   Gb13

#362 Dominant seventh with chromatic embellishment ascending in minor 3rds

#363 Four-note diatonic pattern on dominant sevenths descending in minor thirds

#364 Pattern on dominant 7ths ascending chromatically

#365 Intervallic pattern on dominant 13ths, ascending chromatically

#366 Dominant 7th phrase with chromatic neighbor notes, descending in whole steps

#367 Upper structure arpeggio on dominant 7th (7 to 13), ascending chromatically

#368 Dominant 7b5 phrase, ascending chromatically

#369 Dominant 13ths with b9 , ascending chromatically (Tadd Dameron)

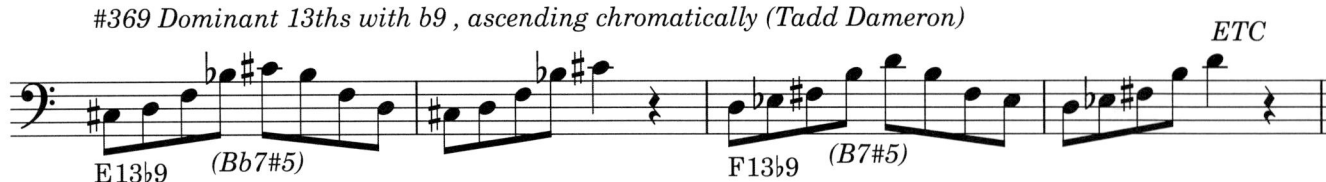

#370 Dominant chords voiced 7 9 3 13, in minor 3rds, each four-chord group separated by a half step

#371 Descending "Diminished Sandwiches"

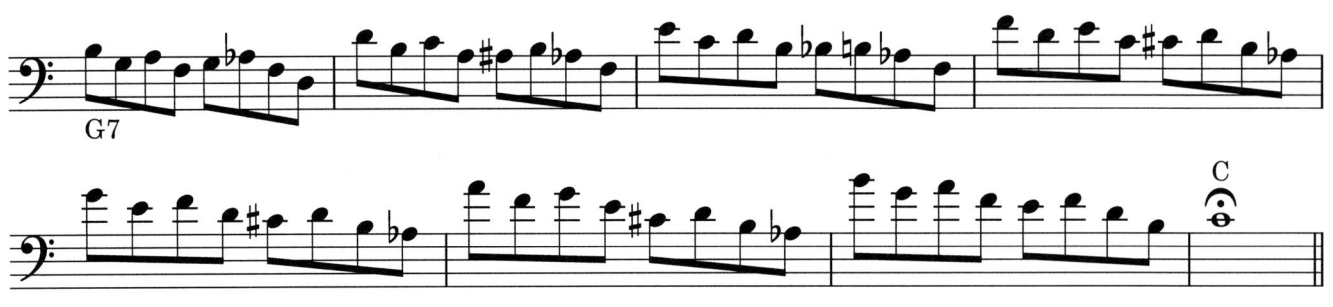

#372 Diminished "sandwiches" coming down a dominant 7th scale resolving to major

#373 Dominant 7 b9 #11 13 descending arpeggios, ascending chromatically

#374 Same as #373, but ascending arpeggios

#375 7 b9 #11 13 ascending arpeggios, ascending in minor 3rds

#376 7 b9 #11 13 descending arpeggios, descending in minor 3rds

#377 Four descending chromatics to b9 #9 ascending in minor 3rds

#378 Same as #377, descending in minor 3rds

#379 Four ascending chromatics to 7 3 9 of dominant, ascending chromatically

#380 Four ascending chromatics to 7 #9 b9 ascending in minor 3rds

#381 Dominant 13th chords, ascending chromatically

#382 Dominant 7th chords with chromatics to #9 b9. ascending in minor 3rds

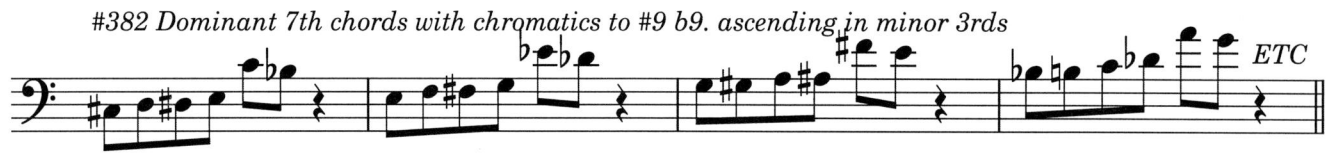

#383 Descending altered dominant arpeggios, in groups of 5, ascending chromatically

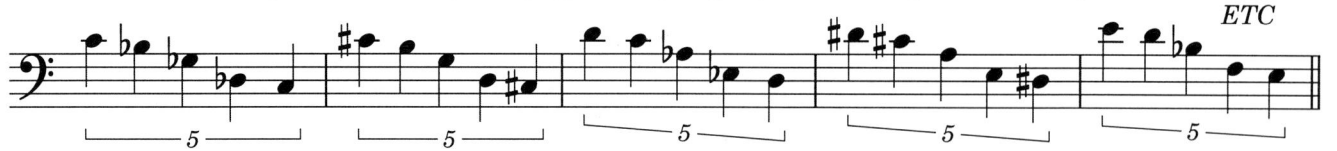

#384 The inverse of #383

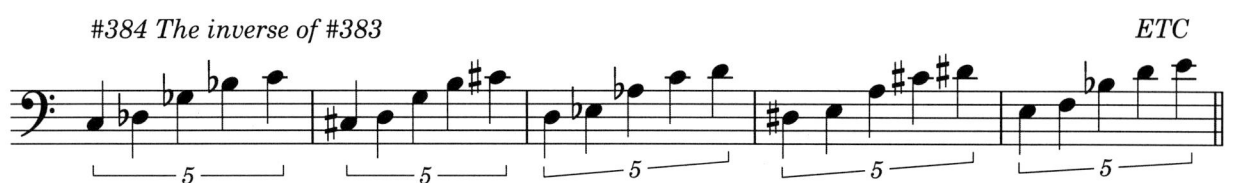

#385 Like #383 and #384, in alternating directions

#386 Dominant 13b9 descending in minor 3rds

#387 Dominant 13b9 ascending chromatically

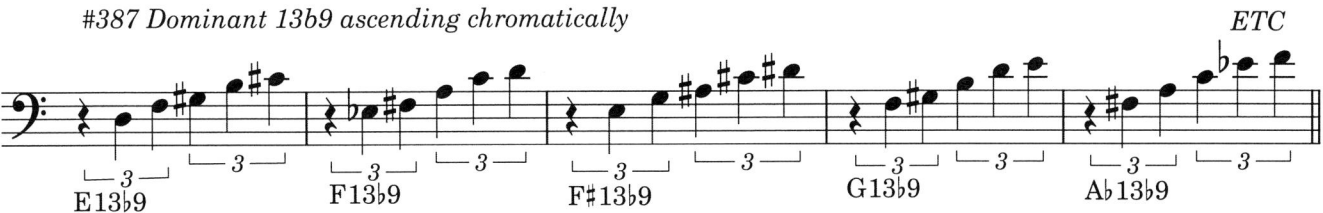

#388 Descending altered dominant pattern

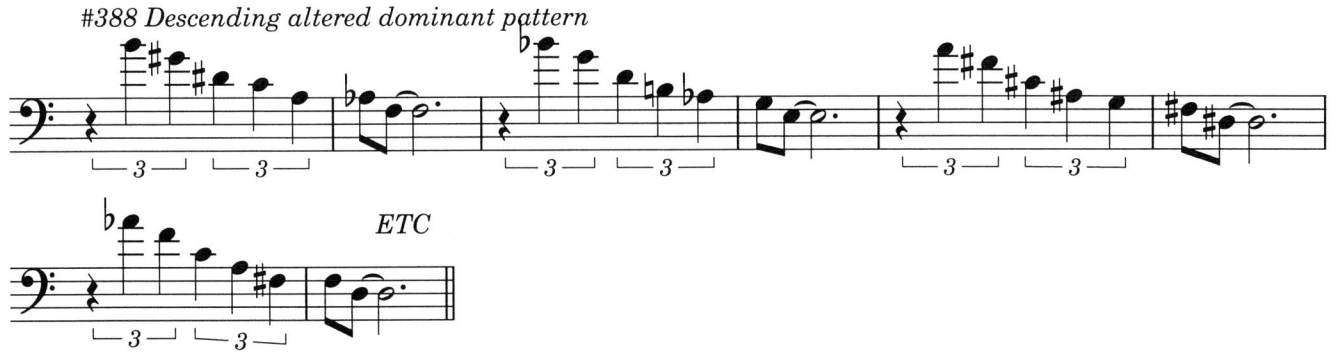

#389 Permutation of dominant 7th chords, ascending chromatically

#390 1st inversion dominant 7th arpeggios with neighbor note, up and down, ascending chromatically

#391 V7#9 descending chromatically

#392 "Spirals" on dominant 7ths, ascending chromatically

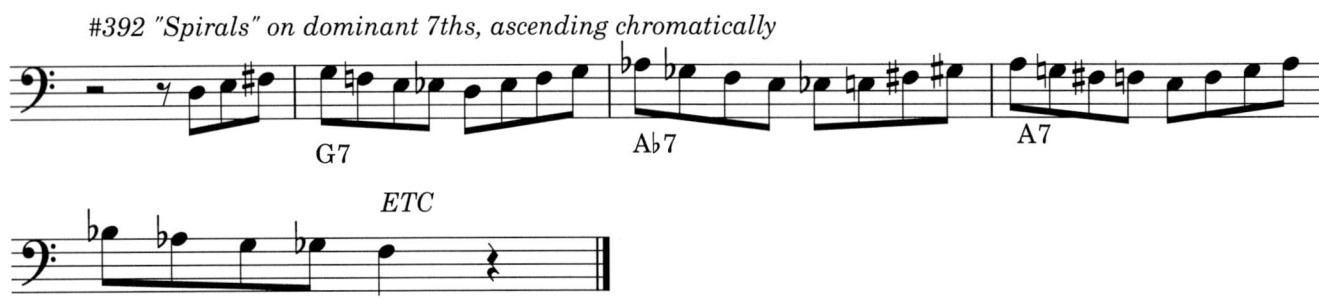

Section 7: Quartals

#393 Quartal triad triplets, ascending chromatically

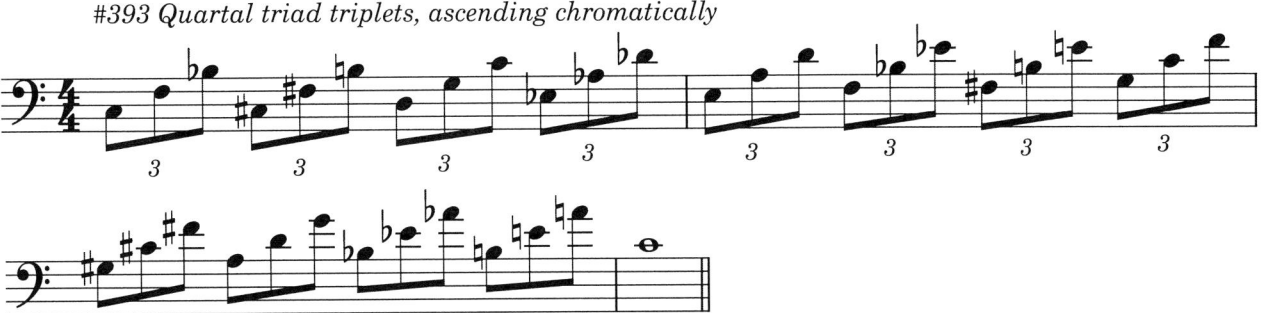

#394 Descending 4th patterns a tritone apart

#395 descending 4ths in 5-note patterns a tritone apart

#396 Quartal triad triplets ascending & descending in minor 3rds

#397 Quartal triad triplets, ascending in whole steps

#398 Ascending 4ths, descending in whole steps

#399 Variations on 4ths and 5ths descending in whole steps

#400 Quartal triads in minor 3rds, used on V7 to I

#401 Quartal triads ascending in whole steps

#402 Quartal triads descending in whole steps

#403 4ths (pentatonic) exercise, ascending chromatically

#404 Quartal triads, ascending in whole steps

#405 Quartal triads, descending in whole steps

#406 Groups of five ascending 4ths, ascending chromatically

#407 Groups of five descending 4ths, ascending chromatically

The Sher Music Co. Catalog
VISIT SHERMUSIC.COM FOR MORE INFORMATION AND TO ORDER ONLINE

BEST-SELLING BOOKS BY MARK LEVINE
The Jazz Theory Book
The Jazz Piano Book
Jazz Piano Masterclass: The Drop 2 Book
How To Voice Standards at the Piano

THE WORLD'S BEST FAKE BOOKS
The New Real Book - Vol. 1 - C, Bb and Eb
The New Real Book - Vol. 2 - C, Bb and Eb
The New Real Book - Vol. 3 - C, Bb, Eb & Bass Clef

The Real Easy Book - Vol. 1 - C, Bb, Eb & Bass Clef
The Real Easy Book - Vol. 2 - C, Bb, Eb & Bass Clef
The Real Easy Book - Vol. 3 - C, Bb, Eb & Bass Clef
The Latin Real Easy Book - C, Bb, Eb & Bass Clef
Drum Supplement for Real Easy Book - Vol. 1

The Standards Real Book - C, Bb and Eb
The Latin Real Book - C only
The Real Cool Book - Octet charts from the 1950s
The All-Jazz Real Book - with selected audio
The European Real Book - with selected audio
The Best of Sher Music Real Books - C, Bb & Eb
The World's Greatest Fake Book - C only
Jazz Arrangements of Public Domain Songs
The Yellowjackets Songbook - separate parts

LATIN MUSIC BOOKS
Contemporary Latin Jazz Guitar - Vol. 1&2, by Neff Irizarry
Decoding Afro-Cuban Jazz - by Mauleon & Valdes
The Salsa Guidebook - by Rebeca Mauleón
101 Montunos - by Rebeca Mauleón
The Latin Bass Book - by Oscar Stagnaro & Chuck Sher
The Latin Real Book - C only
The True Cuban Bass - by Carlos del Puerto
The Brazilian Guitar Book - by Nelson Faria
Inside the Brazilian Rhythm Section - Faria/Korman
Conga Drummer's Guidebook - by Michael Spiro
Language of the Masters - by Michael Spiro
Introduction to the Conga Drum DVD - by M. Spiro
Afro-Caribbean Grooves for Drumset - JPhi Fanfant
Afro-Peruvian Percussion Ensemble - H. Morales
Flamenco Improvisation - Vol.1-3 by Enrique Vargas
Muy Caliente! - Afro-Cuban Book & Play-Aong audio
Music of the Arará Savalú Cabildo - Galvin & Spiro

DIGITAL FAKE BOOKS
The New Real Book - Vol.1 - C, Bb & Eb
The Digital Standards Songbook - individual songs with lyrics, plus C, Bb, Eb, High Voice & Low Voice
The Digital Real Book (650 songs from all our books)

THE DIGITAL SONGBOOK SERIES
The Kenny Barron Songbook
The Carla Bley Songbook
The Tom Harrell Songbook
The Oscar Hernandez Songbook
The Alan Pasqua Songbook
The Horace Silver Songbook
The Steve Swallow Songbook
The Ralph Towner Songbook
The Wayne Wallace Songbook
The Kenny Werner Songbook
The Randy Brecker Songbook
The Larry Dunlap Songbook
The Barry Finnerty Songbook
The Benny Golson Songbook
The Steve Khan Songbook
The Doug Morton Songbook
The Andy Narell Songbook
The Enrico Pieranunzi Songbook
The Dave Tull Songbook
The Denny Zeitlin Songbook

FOR STUDENT MUSICIANS
The Real Easy Book - Vol. 1 - C, Bb, Eb & Bass Clef
The Real Easy Book - Vol. 2 - C, Bb, Eb & Bass Clef
The Real Easy Book - Vol. 3 - C, Bb, Eb & Bass Clef
The Latin Real Easy Book - C, Bb, Eb & Bass Clef
Drum Supplement for Real Easy Book - Vol. 1
The Blues Scales - C, Bb, Eb, Bass Clef & Guitar
Rhythm First! - C, Bb, Eb & Bass Clef - by Tom Kamp
Guitarist's Introduction to Jazz - by Randy Vincent
Walking Bassics - by Ed Fuqua
Foundation Exercises for Bass - by Chuck Sher

CDs
Poetry+Jazz: A Magical Marriage - by Chuck Sher
Play-Along CDs for The New Real Book - Vol.1
The Latin Real Book Sampler CD

Sher Music Co. — JAZZ METHOD BOOKS
available in both print & digital forms

GUITAR
- **Jazz Guitar Voicings: The Drop 2 Book** - Randy Vincent
- **Three-Note Voicings and Beyond** - Randy Vincent
- **Line Games** - Randy Vincent
- **Jazz Guitar Soloing: The Cellular Approach** - Randy Vincent
- **The Guitarist's Introduction to Jazz** - Randy Vincent
- **Contemporary Latin Jazz Guitar, Vol. 1&2** - Neff Irizarry
- **The Jimmy Raney Book** - Jimmy and Jon Raney

PIANO
- **The Jazz Piano Book** - Mark Levine
- **Jazz Piano Masterclass: The Drop 2 Book** - M. Levine
- **How To Voice Standards at the Piano** - Mark Levine
- **An Approach to Comping - Vol. 1** - Jeb Patton
- **An Approach to Comping - Vol. 2** - Jeb Patton
- **Introduction to Jazz Piano: A Deep Dive** - Jeb Patton
- **Playing for Singers** - Mike Greensill
- **Wisdom of the Hand** - Marius Nordal
- **The Jazz Solos of Chick Corea** - Peter Sprague

SAXOPHONE
- **The Practice Notebooks of Michael Brecker**
- **The Jazz Saxophone Book** - Tim Armacost
- **Logic and Critical Thinking in Jazz Improvisation** - Vincent Herring

VOICE
- **The Digital Standards Songbook** - individual songs with lyrics, plus C, Bb, Eb, High Voice & Low Voice
- **The Jazz Singer's Guidebook** - David Berkman

DRUMS
- **Syncopation Companion** - Bryan Bowman
- **Inner Drumming** - George Marsh
- **Drum Supplement for Real Easy Book Vol.1** - Alan Hall
- **Afro-Caribbean Grooves for Drumset** - JPhi Fanfant

BASS
- **The Improvisor's Bass Method** - Chuck Sher
- **Concepts for Bass Soloing** - Marc Johnson & C. Sher
- **Walking Bassics** - Ed Fuqua
- **Foundation Exercises for Bass** - Chuck Sher
- **Walking Bass Line Construction** - Bob Sinicrope — F Blues, Bb Blues and C minor Blues
- **Bass Foundations** - Chuck Israels

Sign up for our monthly discount newsletter by writing shermuse@sonic.net

JAZZ THEORY AND HARMONY
- **The Jazz Theory Book** - Mark Levine
- **The Jazz Harmony Book** - David Berkman
- **Forward Motion** - Hal Galper
- **Metaphors for the Musician** - Randy Halberstadt
- **Minor is Major!** - Dan Greenblatt
- **Rhythm Changes Guide** - Lukas Gabric
- **Jazz Scores and Analysis - Vol.1** - Richard Lawn
- **Jazz Scores and Analysis - Vol. 2** - Richard Lawn
- **The Blues Scales** - C, Bb, Eb, Bass Clef & Guitar - Dan Greenblatt
- **Logic and Critical Thinking in Jazz Improvisation** - Vincent Herring
- **Major is Harmonic** - Randy Vincent

PRACTICE GUIDES
- **The Practice Notebooks of Michael Brecker**
- **Jazz Musician's Guide to Creative Practicing** - David Berkman
- **The Serious Jazz Practice Book** - Barry Finnerty
- **The Serious Jazz Book II** - Barry Finnerty
- **Building Solo Lines from Cells** - Randy Vincent
- **365 Days of Practice** - Rick Margitza
- **Bob Mover Jazz Lexicon** - 2nd edtion - Bob Mover - Bass & Treble Clef versions

EAR TRAINING
- **The Real Easy Ear Training Book** - Roberta Radley
- **Reading, Writing and Rhythmetic** - Roberta Radley

TRUMPET
- **New Orleans Trumpet** - Jim Thornton
- **Modern Etudes for Solo Trumpet** - Cameron Pearce

RHYTHM SECTION GUIDES
- **Essential Grooves** - Moretti, Stagnaro & Nicholl
- **Inside the Brazilian Rhythm Section** - Nelson Faria & Cliff Korman
- **The Salsa Guidebook** - Rebeca Mauleõn
- **Decoding Afro-Cuban Jazz** - Mauleõn & Valdes

BILINGUAL OR LIBROS EN ESPANOL
- **101 Montunos** - Rebeca Mauleõn
- **Muy Caliente!** - Afro-Cuban Book & Play-Along
- **El Libro del Jazz Piano** - Mark Levine
- **The Latin Real Book** - C only

MISCELLANEOUS
- **Method for Chromatic Harmonica** - Max de Aloe
- **Jazz Songs for the Student Violinist** - Kevin Mitchell & Joanne Keefe

ISBN 979-8-9922263-0-0